The Divine Science

THE
DIVINE SCIENCE

ETERNAL TECHNIQUES OF
AUTHENTIC MYSTICISM

A COLLECTION OF:

LOGOS MANTRA THEURGY,

THE ESOTERIC TREATISE OF THEURGY,

AND

THE SEVEN WORDS

Samael Aun Weor

GLORIAN
2009

The Divine Science
A Glorian Book / 2009

Originally published in Spanish as three separate books:
Logos, Mantram, Teurgia (1959)
Tratado Esoterico de Teurgia (1959)
Las Siete Palabras (1953)

ISBN 978-1-934206-40-9

Glorian Publishing is a non-profit organization delivering to humanity
the teachings of Samael Aun Weor. All proceeds go to further the
distribution of these books. For more information, visit our website.

gnosticbooks.org
gnosticteachings.org
gnosticradio.org
gnosticschool.org
gnosticstore.org
gnosticvideos.org

Contents

Logos Mantra Theurgy

Esoteric Treatise of Theurgy

The Seven Words

Introduction

The fundamental basis of all religions is that the divine can be experienced, and it is this notion that you will find emphasized throughout the teachings of Gnosis. Mere belief cannot create anything in life, only action can, and it is here that we must begin our spiritual development: through conscious action, within. This leads us to the very meaning of the word Gnosis: personal knowledge acquired through experience. The true Gnostic does not believe, he *knows* because he has experienced it. As the founder of the modern Gnostic movement, Samael Aun Weor taught and wrote from experience, and expressly demanded that belief and theory be flexible so that the consciousness is free of any restrictions in its effort to reunite with its divine source.

Throughout his more than seventy books, Samael Aun Weor provided an incredible array of practical techniques to aid the serious spiritual devotee to awaken their consciousness. His mission to put the tools in our hands is perhaps most evident in this collection of three books, notably *Logos Mantra Theurgy*. The work to develop the consciousness is the greatest and most worthy endeavor in life, and it is also the most difficult. In this book you will find a priceless collection of tools and armaments to aid you in your journey.

These writings are worthless if they remain merely contemplated or discussed, for their true value can only be known by putting our consciousness into action; the tools given herein will only work in this context. In other words, if you remain theorizing, believing or disbelieving, asleep, inert, in spiritual darkness, the words you read here will remain lifeless. Yet, if you make the effort to awaken your consciousness from moment to moment, and combine that effort with the incredible tools in this book, you will undoubtedly experience life in a whole new way, and with persistence discover the very purpose of your being. It is for this that all of the scriptures and spiritual treatises have been written: for you to awaken to the truth within you.

The sacred words (mantras) given in this book are generally pronounced as they are read, with the vowel sounds similar to those in the Spanish language: I as in "tree," E as in "test," A as in "tall," O as in "low," and U as in "rule."

In the back of this book you will find a short glossary of terms utilized in the Gnostic tradition. If you encounter terms or concepts that require further elucidation, visit GNOSTICTEACHINGS.ORG for an extensive glossary, online courses, articles, audio lectures, and more.

Logos Mantra Theurgy

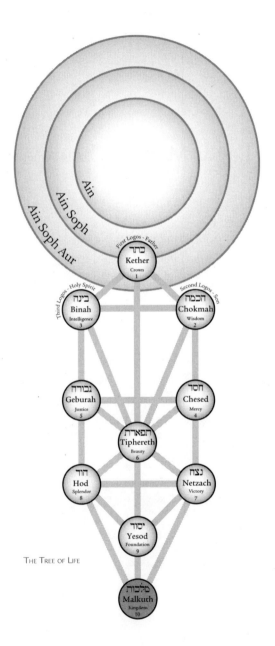

The Tree of Life

1: The Logos

Invocation: The Holy Spirit

We knew a man named John. He was an excellent theurgist! He knew how to consciously travel in his "Astral Body."

One night, a most peaceful, silent night, John left his physical body, and invoked the Holy Spirit... Suddenly a marvelous bird, a white dove of ineffable whiteness, with the head of a venerable elder and a long white beard, deliciously floated above the head of the theurgist. This big and beautiful, pure dove, with the head of a venerable elder, was something to see and admire! The white dove settled upon the shoulders of John's friend, and chanted wise counsel in his ear. Later, the dove of ineffable whiteness, with the head of a venerable elder, stood before John. Enraptured in ecstasy, John as a good disciple, questioned the Holy Spirit: "Oh my Lord, my God, tell me... how am I doing? ... Am I doing well?"

The white dove, taking the shape of a sublime human figure, filled with love, spoke: "My son, you are not doing well!"

Surprised, John asked again: "Lord, tell me, why am I not doing well?"

And the Holy Spirit declared: "I am healing one of your patients, an ill woman who is your responsibility. Thus, you are not the one healing her. I am the one doing it, and yet you have charged her money! That money you received should be returned. It was given to you with much sacrifice on her part!"

In consternation, John answered: "Lord, if I return that money, will I then be on the right path?"

The venerable elder affirmed: "Yes, then you will be doing well, very well!"

The Holy Spirit, the Third Logos (Binah)

John embraced his venerable elder, enraptured in an immense love. The elder blessed John and left. The theurgist knew that this was his own Holy Spirit! He knew that this was

Binah, the Third Logos. Undoubtedly, every human has his white and ineffable dove.

The Logos is the Perfect Multiple Unity.

And the Holy Spirit is the Third Logos.

The prodigious force of the Third Logos flows in the entire Universe.

We have been created by the Third Logos!

Liberation of the Energy of the Third Logos

The human being must liberate the energy of the Third Logos from within his obscure animal depths and make it return "inward and upward," transformed into a torrent of liquid fire.

The Kundalini ascends through the central canal of the spinal medulla until it reaches the top of the head. This is the creative energy of the Third Logos!

The Second Logos (Chokmah)

Another night, John projected his Self within the Astral Body; thus he left his physical body. Then, while outside of his physical body, he withdrew his Self from all of his internal vehicles. He withdrew his Self from within his seven bodies. This is only possible through a supreme ecstasy.

This is how John hovered within that second mediator principle known by Kabbalists as Chokmah, which is the Second Logos, the Perfect Multiple Unity.

Experience within the Venustic Initiation

While in a state of supreme beatitude, John decided to study that Venustic Initiation that the Divine Master received in the Jordan. The outcome was portentous, marvelous. John saw his Self converted into Jesus Christ. He felt his Self being Jesus Christ! Thus, he approached John the Baptist. He entered a marvelous temple. The temple was located at the banks of the Jordan River. This was the temple of the Baptist. Therefore, John, transformed into Jesus Christ, approached the Baptist. This Great Precursor ordered John (transformed into Jesus Christ) to get rid of his robe; John obeyed. John felt absolutely sure of being Jesus Christ himself; there was not one atom of doubt within him!

The Baptist was dressed in his priestly robes. He opened up a type of tabernacle, within which he had two sacred cups: one of oil and the other of wine. The Baptist took out a jar of olive oil and ordered John (transmuted into Jesus) to enter the sanctuary. Once inside, the Baptist anointed John (transmuted into Jesus) with pure oil and sprinkled water on his head. At that precise moment, the shining Dragon of Wisdom, the Internal Christ, entered Jesus (who was John) precisely through the pineal gland located on the upper part of his head. At that moment, the Sun of the Father (the First Logos), the Sun of the Son (the Second Logos), and the Sun of the Holy Spirit (the Third Logos) glowed in the infinite space!

Transmutation into Jesus Christ

Such a marvelous "Seity," that Internal Christ, glowed with immense and absolute whiteness within the internal vehicles of Jesus. Thereafter, the Priest ordered Jesus to sit on a special chair; thus, from that moment on, Jesus was called Jesus Christ! When John returned from such a state of profound ecstasy, he comprehended that in the world of the Second Logos (the World of the Christ), individuality, personality, and the "I" do not exist. Within the World of the Lord, we are all absolutely **one**!

The world of the Second Logos is the central sun.

The Ancient of Days: The First Logos

On another profound and silent night, John (by taking advantage of that transitory moment between vigil and sleep) arose from his bed and the outcome of this action was the conscious projection of John within his Astral Body; thus, he moved joyfully and happily. Suddenly he felt attracted towards the South Pole, towards the continent of Antarctica. John, floating deliciously within the astral plane, arrived at the glacial regions of the South Pole. When the theurgist raised his eyes to the infinite, he saw a Star shining, filled with glory. That Star sparkled marvelously. Within his consciousness, John felt that this Star was calling him, thus he soared through outer space and reached it, and behold the Star was the Ancient of the Days, the Father who is in secret, his own venerable Old Man!

Indeed, within the depths of our consciousness, each of us has a venerable Old Man; he is the First Logos. The Kabbalists call him Kether, the Goodness of Goodness.

The Old Man entered the Soul of John, and the latter felt his Self transfigured. Thus, he saw himself surrounded by an immense aura which encircled the entire planetary globe. The theurgist walked; he was inebriated with a type of happiness impossible to describe with words.

When John returned to his physical body, he comprehended that in the World of the First Logos, individuality and personality do not exist, nor any type of superior or inferior "I."

The Holy Four

The Resplendent Dragon of Wisdom is the Crown of Life; it is the Ray from which our Innermost, the Monad, emerged. The Resplendent Dragon of Wisdom is triune.

John had read that the Trinity within the Unity forms the Holy Four, the Tetragrammaton (Image). However, in spite of having read it, he had not fully comprehended it. With his understanding he had only penetrated within the meaning of the Trinity, but something else was missing; he wanted to integrate the Holy Four into his comprehension!

The Ain Soph

On another night, John discarded every desire, every thought, every will, every consciousness, every ideology, and every preconception; thus, like a breath enraptured in ecstasy, he came out of his physical body through the pineal gland. He then saw himself, converted into an immaculate, ineffable, and divine white atom! Such an atom is the Ain Soph, which is the atom from where the Father, the Son, and the Holy Spirit emanated. When the Great Cosmic Night arrives, the Shining Dragon of Wisdom (Kether, Chokmah, and Binah) of every human being will be immersed within the Ain Soph. Behold here the Trinity immersing within the Unity! Lo and behold the Holy Four, the Tetragrammaton of the Kabbalists!

The Superior Beings of the Ain Soph

John, while enraptured in such a state of ecstasy, knew that deep within each one of us there exists a Star from the infinite space, an ineffable super divine atom of the abstract space.

All of a sudden within the depths of that starry space, John perceived a divine ineffable temple of the Abstract Absolute Space.

John entered through the doors of that sanctuary. Some Gnostic Archbishops were within the temple; John consulted one of them and asked something he needed to know (it was about the exact date of his Cosmic Initiation). The answer was exact, thus the outcome pleased him. Subsequently, he consulted about a few other things regarding the destiny of mankind, and something about his own nemesis (karma). The great Gnostic Archbishop, a holy and venerable Elder, answered: "For us, all of the activities of the human mind are similar to what the activities of the mineral kingdom are to ye; when we examine the human mind, it is like examining a mineral."

John became terribly astounded with such an answer. Indeed, the beings who live within the World of the Ain Soph have transcended us, they are beyond our comprehension. Those beings no longer belong to the human kingdom, not even to the Kingdom of Angels, Seraphim, or Potentates!

Regarding the aforementioned statements, a friend of ours made the following supposition:

The Impossibility of Those Superior Beings

"Let us suppose, if those ineffable and superior beings live immersed within the contemplation of their divine atmosphere, within the Abstract of the Superior Worlds (the world of the **Ain Soph**), then they cannot comprehend us, and it is absolutely impossible for them to descend to us, the humans, since their matter is incompatible with ours."

Reincarnation of Those Beings

We, then, had to answer our friend with the following: "Certainly, each life-form lives in his own element. The fish live in the water; the birds live in the air; humans and terrestrial animals live on the dust of the earth, the salamanders live in the fire. The tenebrous ones exist within the Abyss. And of course, divine hierarchies live in the superior planes of consciousness; yes, they live in the ineffable worlds! The human Monad was an ant, a reptile, bird, and quadruped. It would be impossible for a human to be an ant, reptile, bird, or quadruped again. A human being has already gone through that course and cannot retrograde! The same applies to the ineffable beings of the world of the **Ain Soph**. Neither can they retrogress, nor return to the human state! It would be like humans becoming ants again. Nevertheless, every now and then, some of those beings of Light descended from that elevated region to help mankind. They are the great Avatars, the great reformers, who from the dawn of times, have watched over humanity. In fact, we have not been abandoned. The great White Lodge, with numerous Masters, is here on the terrestrial world; they work on behalf of mankind."

Incarnation of the Logos and of the Kundalini

To incarnate the Logos within our Self is the most essential task. To achieve the Venustic Initiation is what is transcendental and let it be understood that this problem is absolutely sexual!

Every individual needs to awaken the Kundalini; every human being needs to make their creative energy return inwardly and upwardly! When the creative energy reaches the Ethereal Body, the latter is transformed into the wedding garment of the Soul. The chakras awaken when the creative energy breaks through the Astral Body; thus, this is how the person, the student is converted into a true theurgist. Then, the powers of the mind are awakened when this energy reaches the Mental Body. This is how the human mind becomes a Christic Mind.

The human will is transformed into Christic Will when the creative energy rises to the Causal Body, or the Manas of Theosophy. When the creative energy ascends to the Body of Consciousness (Buddhic Body), the Christ Consciousness is originated. Finally, when the creative energy of the Third Logos ascends to the Innermost, we become Creative Gods! This is how we are now prepared to incarnate the **Christ**.

This is how the Word can become Flesh!

The secret clue for this task is the "Arcanum A.Z.F." The clue of the Magnus Opus (the **Great Work**) if found in the union of the phallus and the uterus! Not to ejaculate the ens seminis (the entity of semen) is the vital matter of the clue; this is how the sexual transformation is achieved. This is how the Kundalini awakens! The fires of the dorsal spine are Jehovistic, the fires of the heart are Christic and the Rays of the Father flash on the forehead!

That is why we must sublimate the sexual energies up to the heart, because the Second Logos, the Internal Christ, is located in the heart!

What is from "**above**" must penetrate into that which is from "**below**," so that what is from below can return towards the worlds of Great Light. It is necessary to work with the raw-matter of the Great Work; but this raw-matter, this Christonic semen, must be sublimated up to the heart, only then can the creative energy of the Third Logos be able to elevate itself "**upwards**," towards the worlds of the Great Light. And only then is it possible to become a theurgist!

*"And it shall come to pass, that when they make a long
blast with the ram's horn, and when ye hear the sound of
the trumpet, all the people shall shout with a great shout;
and the wall of the city shall fall down flat, and the people
shall ascend up every man straight before him."*

- Joshua 6:5

2: Mantra

The Universal Sound

Any motion is coessential to sound. Wherever motion exists, sound too exists. The human ear is only capable of perceiving a limited number of sound vibrations. Nonetheless, above and below the sound vibrations that the human ear can perceive, there exist multiple sound waves that the human ear is not capable of perceiving (i.e. the fish of the sea produce their own peculiar sounds). The ants communicate among themselves by means of sounds that are inaudible to our range of physical perception. Sounding waves, acting upon the water produce the motion of elevation and the pressure of the waters. Sounding waves, acting upon the air, produce concentric movements. The atoms spinning around their nuclear centers produce certain sounds that are imperceptible to humans. Fire, air, water, and earth have their own particular sounding notes.

The Keynote and the Seven Vowels

The keynote and the seven vowels of Nature: I-E-O-U-A-M-S, resound in all of creation! Each flower, each mountain, each river, has its own peculiar note, its note synthesis. The combination of all sounds that are produced in the planetary globe produces a note synthesis in the immense core of the infinite space. Thus, each world has its own keynote. The combination of all the keynotes of the infinite forms the ineffable orchestration of the starry spaces; this is the Music of the Spheres of which Pythagoras spoke.

Vibratory Affinity

If a musician playing an instrument was to play the keynote of a man and prolong that note to the maximum, then, that man would die instantly because all of the cells of the human organism are sustained by the sound, by the Word. The atoms of the entire organism live in incessant motion. All that is in motion makes a sound, thus, the Logos sounds; therefore the note synthesis of every atomic movement of the human organism could (by the law of vibratory affinity) kill a human being instantly.

It is written (Joshua 6:5) that when seven priests made a long blast with seven rams' horns trumpets, the walls of Jericho fell down flat, because they played the keynote of those walls. In the army, it is known that when a battalion is going to cross a bridge, they should break the march so as not to destroy the stability of the bridge with their rhythmic sounding march. If the note of a piano is played, and if there is another in tune piano nearby, the latter will repeat the same note as the former. This is due to the law of vibratory affinity.

Apply the former paragraph's examples to the first case we mentioned. Indeed, if the musician was to produce the keynote of a man and prolonged it exceedingly, then, by the law of vibratory affinity, the phenomenon of the two pianos would repeat itself within the organism of that man; thus, this would mean instant death to him, in other words, this would be a very intense commotion beyond the resistance of the normal equilibrium of the structure of that man.

Geometry of the Word

The word produces objective geometric figures. These geometric figures crystallize materially when they are endowed with cosmic matter. "In the beginning was the Word, and the Word was with God, and the Word was God... All things were made by him..!" [John 1:1] The geometric figures of words are concretely recorded on a magnetic tape for use in recording sound. Thus, it is enough to pass the needle over the recording tape for all the words pronounced by the speaker to resound with intensity again.

Mantras

When phonetic combinations are made with wisdom, mantras are produced. Therefore, a mantra is a wise combination of letters whose sounds determine spiritual, psychic, and also physical effects.

Before all the languages of the Tower of Babel were scattered upon the face of the Earth, only one language, a language of Gold, a universal idiom existed. That language has its perfect cosmic grammar. The letters of that golden language are written within all of Nature. Whosoever has studied the Nordic Runes and the Hebrew, Chinese, and Tibetan characters will be able to intuit such a "cosmic language" with its enigmatic letters.

Sexual - Laryngeal Relationship

An intimate relationship between the sexual glands and the creative larynx exists. When a young man reaches the age of fourteen, his voice is transformed into the voice of a mature man. Such a transformation is due to the hormone-releasing activity of his sexual glands. Therefore, the intimate relationship between the sexual glands and the creative larynx is incontrovertible!

The Arcanum A.Z.F. and the Third Logos

The energy of the Third Logos flows through the sexual organs and through the creative larynx. These are the two instruments through which the powerful creative energy of the Third Logos flows. When one works with the "Arcanum A.Z.F.," the sacred serpent is awakened. The ascending current of the creative energy of the Third Logos is living fire. This Pentecostal Fire rises along the medullar canal, opening centers and awakening miraculous powers.

The Christified Word is Sexual

The human being can create with the power of the Word when the sacred fire reaches the creative larynx. In the Internal Worlds, the initiate can think about something and then create it with the Word. The Word creates! The universe was created by the Army of the Voice, by the Great Word!

Those who practice Sexual Magic, those who work with the "Arcanum A.Z.F." must Christify the Word. The Word and sex are intimately related; the Word is sexual! Thus, when someone works with the Magnus Opus, when those individuals transmute their creative energies, they must Christify their language. Vulgar, inharmonious, or arrhythmic words modify the creative energy with their vibrations, giving it absolutely fatal types of vibrations.

Yet, divine words, sublime, harmonic, rhythmic, melodious, and perfect words produce sexual transmutations endowed with glory. Our adorable Savior of the World Christified his Word by drinking from the chalice of sexuality. This is why the Word is mantric! This is why the Word is sexual!

If we were to speak the golden language, then the fire, air, water, and earth would obey us. We would then be authentic Gods! If we were to speak to a mountain in the sacred language, and command the mountain to disintegrate, then the mountain would burst asunder into pieces in a frightening cataclysm.

Deformation of the Word

The sound of the cannon, its explosion, destroys the glass of a window. On the other hand, a soft word calms anger. However, a rude and inharmonious word produces anger, or melancholy, sadness, hatred. It is stated that silence is golden; however it is better to state that: It is wrong to speak when one should be silent, as well as to be silent when one should speak!

There exist fraudulent silences; there exist iniquitous words. The outcome of our spoken words should be calculated with nobility, since many times we hurt others with words uttered unconsciously. Words filled with ill-intended or double meaning produce fornications in the World of the Mind. Angry words engender violence in the World of the Cosmic Mind. One must never condemn anyone with the word, because one must never judge anyone. Slander, gossip, and lies have filled the world with pain and bitterness.

When we work with the "Arcanum A.Z.F.," we must comprehend that the creative energies are exposed to all types of modifications. These energies from our libido can be modified into powers of light or darkness. Everything depends on the quality of our words.

Magical Mantras

Mantras exist for each chakra; occult powers can be awakened with such mantras. Likewise, a great number of mantras exist for Astral Body projection, or in order to attain dominion over the fire, air, water and earth. There also exist mantras that can defend us before the tenebrous entities, which dwell within the Abyss.

For instance: the mantra I... A... O... is the mantra of the "Arcanum A.Z.F."

- I (Ignis, Fire)
- A (Aqua, Water)
- O (Origo, Beginning, Spirit)

The I, the Fire fecundates the A, the Water of universal Genesis, so that life may sprout forth. All this is performed within the O, within the Universal Spirit of Life.

The Internal Master is the "Note Synthesis"

The sacred mysteries of the Logos were known among the Aztecs, Egyptians, Hindus, Persians, Romans, and Greeks, etc. All Hebrew paradises are full of "rivers of pure waters of life" from where flow milk and honey... and of sacred wine, delirium to those who drink it. Indeed, all those sacred rivers, all those waters of life, all those lakes of the temples, are symbols of the Christonic semen which human beings carry within their seminal vesicles. During the esoteric sexual trance, the sacred fire of the Holy Spirit fecundates the waters of life so that the Master may come straight up out of the waters. Certainly, the Internal Master is the note synthesis of all the notes — He is the God that we carry within! He is the Word.

Let Us Vocalize Mantras

The moment to vocalize mantras has arrived. The moment to learn how to spell the golden language to awaken the chakras, or discs, or magnetic wheels of the Astral Body has arrived. Thus, anyone can see, hear, touch and feel the great mysterious realities of the Superior Worlds.

We must get into action, an intentionally supra-physical action, because everything in the universe lives in incessant motion and any motion is coessential to sound. Wherever motion exists, sound also exists! Therefore, let us control the sound!

3: Theurgy

The Priesthood of Theurgy

Theurgy allows us to work in the Superior Worlds.

For instance: Iamblichus was a great theurgist. He knew how to invoke the planetary Gods in order to converse with them.

Theurgy is divine. One cannot become a theurgist without the knowledge of one's Self. The Internal God of every human being is, indeed, the legitimate and authentic theurgist.

There exist three well-defined aspects within the human being: The internal Christ, the Soul, and the Devil.

Who of these three aspects must and can exert the Priesthood of Theurgy?

Let us see:

The "Psychological I" is Satan

The Devil is the "I," is the myself. The Devil is the ego that every human carries within. Such a tenebrous entity is made up of the atoms of the secret enemy.

On a certain occasion, we (some investigators in a group within the Superior Worlds) decided to study that great man named Arnold Krumm-Heller. He wrote numerous books, and died not too long ago (1959). Thus, the investigation was performed when we were out of the physical body.

We invoked Master Krumm-Heller.

Then, the "psychological I," the Satan of Heller, came to our call!

Was the "Psychological I" the Theurgist?

By profoundly analyzing the "psychological I" of Heller, we were able to verify that this "psychological I" was nothing more than a bunch of memories, longings, theories, prejudices, defects, virtues, etc. from his former earthly life. Such a tenebrous entity was wearing a physician's uniform; thus he had the appearance of a great doctor who with a certain resemblance of imposed goodness (between humility and pride) observed us. This was, therefore, the "psychological I," the Satan of that man who was named Arnold Krumm-Heller. Undoubtedly, it is totally impossible for such a "psychological I" to be a theurgist.

When the "psychological I" tries to become a theurgist, he completely fails, because the Devil cannot be a theurgist! The "psychological I" can never be a theurgist!

The "psychological I" can become a necromancer, but a theurgist? This can never happen!

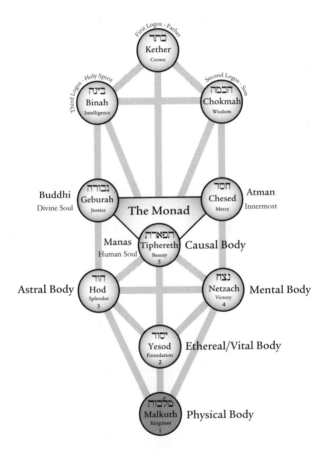

Soul: Atman-Buddhi and Bodhisattva

Now, let us continue with the second aspect: the Soul.

Within the Astral Body, we (the investigating brothers) entered through the doors of the Gnostic Church. There we found two Excellencies seated. The first was the Innermost of Arnold Krumm-Heller who was dressed as a Gnostic Archbishop in archiepiscopal purple, with a miter. The second one was the Bodhisattva of the Master Heller.

The first was the Purusha of the Orientals, the Monad, the Innermost: Atman-Buddhi. The second was the Superior Manas of oriental Theosophy: the Causal Body, or better said, the Willpower-Soul wrapped up with the Mental and Astral Bodies, which constitute that which is called Bodhisattva.

The Theurgist is the Internal Christ

An in-depth analysis of these two Excellencies leads us to the conclusion that, indeed, these are two aspects of the Being, two modifications of the soul of the world: two divine modifications. The soul of the world itself cannot be the celebrant. The soul of the world has to study the rituals of life and death, as the celebrant is arriving.

Therefore, the theurgist is further within; it is deeper, more profound. The theurgist is the Internal Christ of every human that comes into the World. Within the human being, the theurgist is the shining Dragon of Wisdom, which is the Ray from where the very Innermost emanated.

When the Internal God enters the Innermost, a mirific transformation can be contemplated. The Innermost, the soul of the world, suffers a transformation within us, it becomes deified, it becomes absolutely divine. That which is called the Son of Man is derived from this alchemical marriage, from this marvelous combination of divine and human principles. When the Son of Man penetrates within the Bodhisattva, the latter also passes through a miraculous transformation. This is how the theurgist is born within a human being, within us!

The Dissolution of the "I" of the Theurgist

The Initiate who aspires to High Theurgy must first study the rituals of life and death, as the celebrant is arriving. Whosoever wants to reach High Theurgy must decide to die... in order to be, one must dissolve the "I," the myself, Satan!

This work is hard, arduous, and terribly difficult. One must begin with the decapitation of the "I," and the task of dissolving such an "I" is only performed by means of millenarian purifications and based upon profound, creative comprehension.

In the first steps of theurgy, immediate power can be exercised over the Mental, Astral, Ethereal, and even physical planes. The superior steps are infinite and lead up to the Absolute. This process is slow, patient, and methodical.

Theurgy, Science of Gods!

Students should not become discouraged because of the fact that Theurgy is a science for Gods, exclusively for Gods. There is always a step where one begins. Nobody can attend college without first ascending the educational ladder. Therefore, we have to begin by practicing within the Astral Plane. Later, as Iamblichus, one can work and converse with the Sidereal Gods in very elevated worlds.

4: The Angel Aroch

Invocation of Aroch

One night John projected himself out from within his physical body. Undoubtedly, he was skillful in "Astral projection." He knew how to "consciously travel" in his Astral Body... he was a competent investigator of the Superior Worlds. Once out of the physical body, John felt himself invaded by an unutterable spiritual voluptuousness. There is no greater pleasure than to feel the Soul "detached" within the Internal Worlds. There, the past and the future merge within an eternal now! There, time does not exist! Hence, John feeling enraptured and following his own mystical inspiration entered through the doors of a temple.

Thus, this marvelous theurgist invoked the Angel Aroch, Angel of Command. He made the invocation in the following manner:

> *In the name of Christ,*
> *by the power of Christ,*
> *by the majesty of Christ,*
> *I call upon thee Angel Aroch!*
> *Angel Aroch!*
> *Angel Aroch!*

The Tenebrous Ones of Drukpa

The outcome of the invocation was astounding: a few moments later, a beautiful boy of about twelve years old entered through the doors of the temple. This was the Angel Aroch! This angel operates through the Ray of Strength, and works intensely with the disciples who tread the path of Adepthood.

Thus, dressed in a white robe, such a precious creature saluted John and sat at his side, before a table in the temple. John then consulted the Angel about certain things and concurrently, he presented the following complaint: certain tenebrous ones from a school of black magic were horribly defaming the Gnostic teachings.

Such tenebrous ones had a university where they studied the Tantric science of the Drukpa clan, the science of the Tibetan red caps. For this tenebrous Tibetan clan, Shamballa (where the Royal White Lodge lives) is "according to them," a city of terror where the blind fohatic force moves, as well as a thousand other lies!

These people render cult to the goddess Kali and practice the science of the Nicolaitanes, the Tantrism of the tenebrous ones...

Defamation against Gnosticism

The Tao Path leads to final liberation; this is the path of the Gnostic Initiates.

What the tenebrous adepts of the Drukpa clan teach is fatality, the shadow of the Tao Path, the antithesis of the Tao Path.

Therefore, the henchmen of such a secret association were launching improper statements against the Gnostic Movement. John therefore suffered unutterably; this is why he presented the complaint to the Angel Aroch! John also showed the Angel a magazine in which Gnosis was violently attacked. The Angel then took a scale and weighed the good and the evil; thereafter the Angel said: "I will take care of this!"

The outcome was astonishing... a few days later that secret society was dissolved and failed completely.

Mantra for Kundalini

After the above mentioned complaint and the promise of intervention by the Angel, John begged the Angel to teach him the most powerful mantra that exists in the entire universe in order to awaken the Kundalini. The Angel then chanted a marvelous mantra, which moved John. It is as follows:

Kandil Bandil Rrrrrrrr...

VOCALIZATION: The first syllables of each sacred word (KAN and BAN) receive a high intonation, soft and prolonged, while the final syllables of these mantras (DIL and DIL) have a respectively low and prolonged intonation. The intonation of the R receives a harmonious and subtly higher vibration than the first mentioned syllables; it is as if a child was trying to imitate the vibratory hum of a motor in motion, or like hearing the hum of a stone sharpener propelled by an electric motor when sharpening a thin steel blade, this is an acute, high sound, with the tendency of producing flute modulations:

Kaaaaannnnn... Diiiiiiiillllll...

Baaaaannnnn... Diiiiiiiillllll...

Rrrrrrrr...

These mantras can be chanted repeatedly, daily, as many times as possible, throughout long periods of time.

After the Angel Aroch chanted these mantras, John, the theurgist also chanted them and the Angel blessed him. Thereafter, the Angel (carrying the Scale of Justice in his hands along with the hostile magazine which John had shown him) withdrew from the precinct.

"And, behold, the angel of the Lord came upon him, and a light shined in the prison: and he smote Peter on the side, and raised him up, saying, Arise up quickly."

- Acts 12

5: The Jinn State

Mantra and "Jinn"

One day, a great friend of ours, who is dedicated to scientific astrology, was commenting to us about the case of a man, who whenever he was placed into prison, mysteriously disappeared, frustrating the vigilance of his guards! It was useless to chain him down, because he was always able to free himself from any chain and disappear!

This man established a friendship with the astrologer and, finally, did not have any problem in revealing the respective clue, the valuable secret to the astrologer.

Let us look at the clue:

The following mantras must be written on a large loaf of bread:

Senosan Gorora Gober Don

Thereafter, the student eats the bread. The former mantric words must be written in the form of a cross, with a pencil or with an ink pen, etc.

The distribution of these mantras is as follows: Senosan Gorora must be written horizontally; and Gober Don must be written vertically, starting from the top down, perpendicularly, passing through the space left between the first two sacred words.

Investigation of the Clue

After thanking the scientific astrologer that revealed to us the former "Jinn" clue, we decided to investigate on our own in the Superior Worlds, to find out the scientific and esoteric value of this clue.

Thus, to achieve the desired result, we, the investigating brothers, became drowsy by vocalizing these mantras. The outcome was astounding: When we "abandoned" our physical bodies and entered the Astral Plane, we then saw the sea and a terrific God of the ocean causing the unfathomable depths of the sea to shake in a terrifying manner. Ethereal waves were formed which spun concentrically, trying to precipitate themselves with great violence towards the place where we had left the physical body.

Such an outstanding God of the immense sea had provoked the electrical whirlwind, the ethereal hurricane, the terrific force in order to toss it towards the place where we had left the physical body; who knows what were this God's mysterious intentions, however, our terror translated it into a fatality.

Nevertheless, such was the powerful being who would have to come to our call, in order to place our physical body in the "Jinn" state, in order to submerge it within the fourth dimension and thus transport it to any place in the world.

"Jinn" Paradise, the Garden of Delights

Positively, such a God of the water has power over the Ether of Life, and his power is omnipotent... Thus, in this manner we explain to ourselves, the scientific clue which our astrologer friend revealed to us.

Naturally, the Hierarchies, the "Jinn Masters," only grant this type of theurgical operation when the victim is cast unjustly into prison. No Master of the great White Lodge would ever dare to violate the Law!

Therefore, we learn how to place the physical body in "Jinn" State with the power of these mantras, and with that power, many victims can be saved from the pain and injustice of mankind.

In ancient times the humans from the first races lived in the "Jinn" paradises, yet they fell in this dense tridimensional world. Nevertheless, let us learn how to place the physical body in "Jinn" state; thus, we will have the privilege of visiting the "Jinn" Paradises where the rivers of pure water spring forth milk and honey. That is the "Garden of Delights" of which Mohammed spoke. Listen to his words:

These are they who are drawn nigh (to Allah), in the gardens of delights.

A numerous company from among the first and a few from among the latter, on thrones decorated, reclining on them, facing one another.

Round about them shall go youths never altering in age, with goblets and ewers and a cup of pure drink; they shall not be affected with headache thereby, nor shall they get exhausted, and fruits such as they choose, and the flesh of fowl such as they desire.

And pure, beautiful ones, the like of the hidden pearls: A reward for what they used to do.

They shall not hear therein vain or sinful discourse, except the word peace, peace.

And the companions of the right hand; how happy are the companions of the right hand! Amid thorn-less lote-trees, and banana-trees (with fruits), one above another! And extended shade, and water flowing constantly, and abundant fruit, neither intercepted nor forbidden, and exalted thrones!

Surely we have made them to grow into a (new) growth, then we have made them virgins, loving, equals in age. - The Quran, chapter 56: The Event: 11-37

The Bible narrates the case of Peter, who, locked up in prison, managed to escape by placing his physical body in "Jinn" State.

Peter therefore was kept in prison: but prayer was made without ceasing of the church unto God for him.

And when Herod would have brought him forth, the same night Peter was sleeping between two soldiers, bound with two chains: and the keepers before the door kept the prison.

And, behold, the angel of the Lord came upon him, and a light shined in the prison: and he smote Peter on the side, and raised him up, saying, Arise up quickly. And his chains fell off from his hands.

And the angel said unto him, Gird thyself, and bind on thy sandals. And so he did. And he said unto him, Cast thy garment about thee, and follow me.

And he went out, and followed him; and wist not that it was true which was done by the angel; but thought he saw a vision.

When they were past the first and the second ward, they came unto the Iron Gate that leads unto the city; which opened to them of his own accord: and they went out, and passed on through one street; and forthwith the angel departed from him.

And when Peter was come to himself, he said: now I know of a surety, that the Lord hath sent his angel, and hath delivered me out of the hand of Herod, and from all the expectation of the people of the Jews. - Acts 12:5-11

Conclusion

Such is the clue that will allow us to place the physical body in "Jinn State."

We fall into a state of slumber by vocalizing the mantras that we have revealed. Emulating Peter, we will be assisted by an Angel, then we will rise from our bed and walk like somnambulists. This is how our physical body will enter the Garden of Delights, into the "Jinn" Paradises.

6: The Bird of Minerva

The Quetzal

The bird of Minerva is the symbol of wisdom. A good deal has been said about the Quetzal; however, few are capable of understanding the mystery of this sacred bird.

The Quetzal is one of the most beautiful birds of the world. Its green feathered tail is long and very beautiful. Over its head it wears a crest of incomparable green and silky beauty. The entire appearance of this bird invites us to reflect.

The bird of Minerva, the miraculous Quetzal, is the outcome of the incessant transmutations of fire. When the sacred Pentecostal Fire ascends through the central canal of the spinal medulla, it has the miraculous power of transforming itself into a bird of fire. The Quetzal is the symbol of this bird of fire, which is the bird of Minerva.

The secret power of this bird allows any human to become a God! It grants metamorphosis into whatever shape one wishes to be. Likewise, the secret power of this bird has the capacity of opening the chakras, the wheels or magnetic discs of the Astral Body. This is the key to the priestly power.

The "Arcanum A.Z.F." and the Kundalini!

The theurgist can make use of that power when he is working with the "Arcanum A.Z.F."

It has already been stated that in the union of the phallus and the uterus lies the key of all evident power.

Likewise, we have already warned the theurgist that during his life he must never ejaculate the entity of the semen. Thus, this is how by refraining from desire, the seminal liquid is transmuted into subtle magical vapors and in turn, such vapors will convert themselves into electromagnetic Christic energies.

The ascension of these Christic creative energies of the Third Logos is achieved through the ganglionic cords, known in the Orient by the names of Ida and Pingala. These are the two witnesses of Revelation. These two cords entwined around the spinal medulla form the Caduceus of Mercury. The igneous serpent of our magical powers, the sacred fire of Kundalini awakens when the solar and lunar atoms, (which ascend through these two ganglionic cords) make contact in the coccygeal bone near the Triveni. The ascension of the Kundalini is performed throughout the central canal of the spinal medulla. The Kundalini develops, evolves and progresses within the aura of the Solar Logos. The Kundalini ascends slowly according with the merits of the heart. The fires of the heart control the ascension of the Kundalini. Thus, the fire of Kundalini transforms into the bird of Minerva! What is important is to know the clue!

Mantra for "Sexual Magic"

Now, we no longer can deny humanity the key of the powers that deify. Thus, with gladness we deliver this miraculous clue to our disciples.

Very well, during the trance of Sexual Magic, vocalize the following mantra:

Jao Ri

The sound of each vowel is prolonged. The marvelous bird of fire must be commanded to open, to develop the chakra that is needed, to start the total development of the faculty that is needed the most. You can be sure that the bird of Minerva will work on the chakra, the magnetic disc or wheel (upon which it received the supreme orders).

It is evident and positive that those faculties are not developed instantly. Yet, the bird of Minerva will eventually awaken them! If one continues with the practice daily, that bird, the sacred Quetzal, will develop in an absolute manner the ordered and desired faculty. What is important is to persevere, without getting tired, and to practice daily with a fervent intensity.

Projection of the Fire to the Chakras

This miraculous bird of fire provides the clue in order to project the fire of Kundalini at a distance and thus to help the sick or to project the fire to any chakra of the Astral Body of the esotericist.

Some students will project the fire to their prostatic chakra with the goal of attaining the powers of consciously departing and traveling within the Astral Body. Others will do it with the goal of developing clairvoyance (through the frontal chakra). Others will do it in order to gain the power of hearing the ultra (through the chakra of the larynx); this chakra of the larynx enables the yogi to conserve his physical body alive and perfectly healthy, even during the Cosmic Nights. Others will project the bird of Minerva to the solar plexus, which grants the power of remaining within fire for hours without getting burnt. Some students will send the marvelous bird to the heart chakra, which will grant them power over hurricanes, winds, etc. Likewise, the bird of Minerva can be sent to the chakra of one thousand petals, which is located in the superior part of the skull. Such a chakra grants intuition, polyvoyance, intuitive vision, and the power to consciously leave the physical body within the Spirit, our Innermost, without vehicles of any kind.

The bird of Minerva can also be sent to the atoms of the physical body, and to command it to prepare the body for the "Jinn" State.

Thus, all of us must learn how to project the fire to any corner of the universe, and to any chakra of our organism! This is how everyone will awaken their internal powers, because in order to work in the Great Work it is not enough to light the fire, it is necessary to learn how to intelligently employ it.

Restoration, Transformation, and Invisibility

Agni is the God of fire. This great Master helps to restore the fire in each of the seven bodies: Physical, Ethereal, Astral, Mental, Causal, Buddhic, and Atmic.

The theurgist can invoke Agni when he moves about in the Astral Plane. Agni will come to his call. When the theurgist invokes Agni, he will call him as follows:

In the name of the Christ,
By the majesty of Christ,
By the power of Christ.

If before the eyes of his friends, the invoker commands the bird of fire to transform his face or commands the bird to give him a bird's appearance (or that of a tree, etc) the bird will perform the transformation and his friends will not recognize him.

Now then, if we project the bird of fire to the mind of someone who is waiting to harm us, and if we command that person's mind not to see us, we will then become invisible.

But, in this case, we must also vocalize the mantras whose power will make us invisible. They are as follows:

Iod He Vau He Amoa He Vau He A Gta

Often, Jesus, the great Hierophant who taught us Gnosis, had to become invisible.

Innumerable marvels can be learned and executed with the power of the fire. We can transform ourselves radically with the power of the fire. We can become Gods with the power of the fire!

7: The Chakras

The Vowels and the Faculties of the Chakras

In ancient times, the seven vowels of Nature: **I E O U A M S** resounded within the human organism. But, when humanity came out of the "Jinn" lands, rhythm and harmony were lost.

Therefore, the human being must be aware of the urgent necessity for the seven vowels of Nature to vibrate once again within the organism; they must resound with intensity within the resonating internal chambers, as well as in each of the plexus or chakras of the Astral Body.

Clairvoyance is developed with the vowel I.

Clairaudience is awakened with the vowel E.

The heart center that develops inspiration is developed with the vowel O.

The pulmonary chakra that allows us to remember past reincarnations is developed with the vowel A.

The frontal chakra — **I** — Faculty: Clairvoyance.

The larynxean chakra — **E** — Faculty: Magic Ear.

The cardiac chakra — **O** — Faculty: Intuition, astral projections.

The pulmonary chakra — **A** — Faculty: Memory of past lives.

The umbilical chakra — **U** — Faculty: Telepathy.

THE CHAKRAS

The vowels M and S make all of the internal centers vibrate.

These vowels combined with certain consonants integrate the mantras that facilitate the awakening of all the chakras.

Subsequently, here is a series of these mantras:

First Series of Mantras

CHIS: Clairvoyance: Ajna chakra

CHES: Clairaudience: Vishuddha chakra

CHOS: Intuition: heart, Anahata chakra

CHUS: Telepathy: solar plexus, chakra Manipura

CHAS: Memory of past lives: pulmonary chakra

Vocalization

This vocalization must be performed as follows: prolong the sound of each letter; the combination CH (letter Chet) is considerably abundant in Hebrew mantras; it has an immense magical power.

The vocalization of each mantra makes the magnetic center, chakra or disc with which it is related, to vibrate.

The S is intimately connected to fire and is vocalized by giving it a special type of intonation: this is an acute-hissing sound similar to the sound that compressed air brakes of any given machine make.

Second Series of Mantras

IN: Clairvoyance: frontal chakra

EN: Clairaudience: laryngeal chakra

ON: Intuition: heart chakra

UN: Telepathy: solar plexus

AN: Memory of past lives: pulmonary chakra

Vocalization

Prolong the sound of each vowel and give a strong sounding bell-like intonation to the letter N.

Third Series of Mantras

INRI: Clairvoyance: Ajna chakra

ENRE: Clairaudience: Vishuddha chakra

ONRO: Intuition, inspiration: Anahata chakra

UNRU: Telepathy: solar plexus, Manipura chakra

ANRA: Memory of past lives: pulmonary chakra

Vocalization

Vocalize these mantras during the practice of Sexual Magic; prolong the sound of each of the letters that compose them, thus their respective chakras will awaken. The letter R is vocalized as it was explained in chapter 4.

Fourth Series of Mantras

SUIRA: Clairvoyance: frontal chakra

SUERA: Clairaudience: laryngeal chakra

SUORA: Intuition: heart chakra

SUURA: Telepathy: solar plexus

SUARA: Memory of past lives: pulmonary chakra

VOCALIZATION

The student must focus on the accentuation of the vowels and the accentuation of the vowel A in each mantra which forms the fourth series of mantras.

According to the Vedas, the silent Gandharva, the heavenly musician, is contained within the sublime SWARA.

With this fourth series of mantras, the fire of the solar plexus is driven out towards each of the chakras of the Astral Body.

Again, the first mantric syllables of the fourth series of mantras: SUI, SUE, SUO, SUU, SUA are vocalized with the intonation of a diphthong accentuated on the last vowel, which must be prolonged lengthily.

Vocalize the syllable RA of each one of these mantras by giving the R the intonation already explained in chapter four. The vowel of this syllable RA must also be lengthily prolonged.

Insistence on a Few Details

Students must vocalize for one hour daily in order to effectively awaken their chakras. Since every student has their own rhythm, their personal vibration, they will choose any of the four series of mantras mentioned. There will be some students who will feel more confident with the first series, others with the second series, etc.

Dr. Krumm-Heller stated that one hour of daily vocalization was enough. One must vocalize during one's whole life, this in order to keep the chakras in intense activity!

The coronary chakra engenders polyvoyance.

The frontal chakra, located between the eyebrows, engenders Clairvoyance.

The laryngeal chakra, clairaudience.

The heart chakra grants inspiration and intuition.

The solar plexus chakra, telepathy.

The pulmonary chakra allows us to remember past lives.

The prostatic/uterine chakra grants the power to consciously depart in the Astral Body. Every student must possess such a power, if not, it is mandatory for such a student to awaken this chakra.

Exercise for the Prostatic/Uterine Chakra

While focusing on the prostatic/uterine chakra, the disciple must submerge himself into profound meditation. Imagine the chakra as a lotus flower, as a magnetic disc that spins clockwise while vocalizing the letter M, as when a bull begins to bellow but without decreasing the sound of the M and lengthily sustaining it. In order to provoke such a sound, inhale the air deeply then pronounce the M while having the lips hermetically sealed, until the last particle of breath is exhaled, as follows:

Mmmmmmmmmmmmmmmmmmmmmmmm

With these four series of mantras, the student can become a practical theurgist.

8: Astral Travel Experiences

Projection of the Theurgist

The theurgist has to acquire a practical, infallible capacity to consciously project himself in the Astral Body. This capacity must be established as a habit that can be exercised voluntarily at any given moment and under any circumstance; it does not matter if one is alone or before witnesses. Otherwise, one is not a theurgist.

Now, the disciples will learn numerous clues in order to acquire this admirable and precious capacity.

First Clue

The disciple must enter into a slumber state while vocalizing the mantra FARAON, which must be chanted in three syllables, as follows:

Fffffaaaa... Rrrraaaa... Ooooonnnn...

The vocalization of the letter R has already been explained.

The disciple must lie down (horizontally), facing up. Without rigidity, the disciple must extend his arms to either side of his body and place the palms of the hands on the surface of the bed. The knees must be bent, and thus the soles of the feet will rest upon the bed. The entire body must be relaxed, limb by limb.

Thus, in this manner, the disciple must enter into a slumber state and by profoundly breathing, chant the mantra FARAON.

Thus, the disciple (in a slumber state) will inevitably come out of the physical body without knowing how or when.

Now, the disciple's Astral Body will unavoidably be projected within the internal worlds, within the fifth dimension. Here the disciple's consciousness will fully awaken, in other words, his/her consciousness will become aware of the amazing experiences within those worlds and he will be able to dedicate himself to the practice of Theurgy.

Nonetheless, before lying down, one must perform the sign of the Microcosmic Star. To that effect, the arms are raised upwards until the palms of the hands touch each other above the head.

Thereafter, extend the arms laterally so that they remain in a horizontal position, forming a cross with the rest of the body. Finally, cross the forearms (the right over the left) on your chest, touching it with the palms while the fingertips reach the front of your shoulders.

Our adorable Savior of the World, the Christ Jesus, used this mysterious clue (that only now has been revealed to us) when He studied in the Pyramids of Kefren.

Master Huiracocha advises the burning of some aromatic substance, some incense, or simply impregnate your room with a good perfume.

Second Clue

In this second clue, the disciple must enter into a slumber state while vocalizing the mantra: ***Tai Re...Re...Re...***

This mantra must be chanted strongly by accentuating the vowel A: Taaaaaaiiiiiiii.

The three remaining syllables are vocalized by giving onto the E (as pronounced in the word "red") a melodious, pro-longed bell-like sound. Do not roll the R; pronounce it simply:

Reeeeeeee... Reeeeeeeee... Reeeeeeee...

Chant the syllable TAI in a deep tone.

Repeat the syllable RE three times in a higher tone than TAI.

When the disciple is already in a slumber state, (which is that precise state of transition between vigil and sleep) he/she must rise from his/her bed without hesitation, laziness, doubts, or reasoning; he/she must rise naturally as a reflected action or in an instinctive, automatic and absolutely childlike manner. For example, observe the birds: when they are going to fly, they do not reason, they do not harbor doubts or preconceptions, they simply fly away instinctively, we could say, automatically. The disciple must imitate the birds and proceed in this manner. Therefore, he must rise from the bed and leave the room and depart towards any corner, any place of the infinite.

When we state that the student must rise from the bed, this must be translated into effective and immediate action, without thinking about it.

Unforeseen and Reflex Astral Projection

We will now mention the case of a gentleman, who while sleeping, had to unexpectedly get up from his bed in order to open the door of his house (he overheard someone knocking at the door). When he returned to his bedroom he had the tremendous surprise of finding a man sleeping in his bed. By carefully observing the man, he became perfectly aware that the man was his own physical body, which he had left asleep within his bed.

Based on the former reference, the students will be able to realize that when a person gets up from his bed in the precise moment of entering into a slumber state, the outcome is inevitably "an astral projection."

The gentleman of the former paragraph "projected himself into the astral" because he got up from his bed with the most complete spontaneity. The projection happened without mental analysis, fear or prejudgment. He simply got up in order to open the door, and that was all!

Third Clue

A "still, small voice" incessantly resounds within the cells of the human brain. This is a sharp, hissing sound. This is the sound of a "chirping cricket," the "hissing of the serpent," the "Anahat sound." The Voice of Brahma has ten tonalities that the theurgist must learn how to listen to. As the bee absorbs itself within the nectar of the flower, likewise the mind of the student should be absorbed within that sound.

Whosoever wishes to perceive the "Anahat sound," must empty the mind, must quiet the mind, but not forcefully quiet it; we repeat: quiet.

Let us perceive the difference between a mind that is quiet because it has comprehended that it is useless to think and a mind that is artificially quieted. Understand the difference between a mind that attains a spontaneous, natural silence, and a mind that has been silenced by force, violently.

When the mind is quiet, in profound silence, the student can then inevitably perceive the sound of the cricket: a subtle, sharp, penetrating sound. Moreover, if the soul of the student is absorbed within such a mystical sound, then the doors of mystery open up for him. Consequently, in those moments, he can rise from the bed instinctively and leave the room; he can go towards the temples of the White Lodge, or to any place in the universe.

The disciple must learn how to play the lyre of Orpheus. This lyre is the Word, the Sound, the great Word!

Fourth Clue

The disciple must enter into a slumber state while vocalizing the letter S like a still, small hiss: *Sssssssssssssssssssss*.

By vocalizing the letter S, the student will acquire the capacity to resound the still, small voice within his brain, the

Anahat sound at will; this will allow him to consciously project himself in his Astral Body.

Fifth Clue

The sexual energy is bipolarized into positive and negative. The solar atoms from our seminal system ascend through the right ganglionic cord, which entwines around the spinal medulla. Likewise, the lunar atoms from the seminal system ascend through the left ganglionic cord, which entwines around the spinal medulla.

The Solar Atoms resound with the mantra: RA.

The Lunar Atoms vibrate intensely with the mantra: LA.

The sexual power of the two witnesses known in the Orient by the names of Ida and Pingala can be used in order for the still, small voice, the Anahat sound, to resound within the brain.

The Anahat sound is produced by the sexual energies in motion. It is already known that all motion produces sound. Therefore, if we compel the "Solar and Lunar atoms" of our seminal system to vibrate with intensity, then, the Anahat sound will strongly (and with more intensity) resound; this will grant us the capacity to consciously project ourselves in the Astral Body.

Therefore, enter into a slumber state by mentally vocalizing the following:

Laaaaaaaaaa... Raaaaaaaaa...

Laaaaaaaaaa... Raaaaaaaaa...

With these mantras, the above mentioned Solar and Lunar Atoms will intensely spin, forming an electric whirlwind. The spinning movement produces the Anahat sound, which will allow the student to consciously escape from the physical body. It is essential for the student to get up from the bed (while in a slumber state) and take advantage of the mystical sound.

The two witnesses of the Revelation of St. John grant the power of prophecy, because they produce the awakening of the consciousness. The Solar Fire rises through the right ganglionic cord; the Lunar Water rises through the left ganglionic cord. Fire plus water is equal to Consciousness. The fire of Phlegethon and the water of Acheron cross in the Ninth Sphere (Sex), forming the sign of the Infinite. This sign is the Holy Eight. If we carefully observe the Caduceus of Mercury, we perceive the Holy Eight, formed by the two serpents that are entwined around it.

Sixth Clue

Master Huiracocha mentions in his "Rosicrucian Novel," that a prodigious cactus named peyote or jiculi exists in Mexico. He states that this cactus has the power of awakening clairvoyance instantaneously to whosoever masticates it. The peyote allows the conscious projection of the Astral Body.

This is a sacred plant of the grand White Lodge.

Unfortunately, in the capital of the Mexican Republic, it is absolutely impossible to find the authentic peyote. It can only be found in San Luis Potosi or among the Tarahuamara Indians of La Sierra in Chihuahua.

The Masters of the Temple of Chapultepec use this cactus for their instant and urgent astral journeys (all they need is to chew it).

(EDITOR'S NOTE: The following is from *Aztec, Christic Magic*, by the same author: "The Aztec Masters utilized the peyote (peyotl) in order to teach the neophytes to travel in their Astral Bodies. However, we do not recommend the use of this marvelous cactus which makes the Astral Body separate itself from the physical body and preserves the lucidity of consciousness while acting in the Astral world. Indeed, what we recommend is practice, much practice and soon you will act and travel within the Astral Body.")

Seventh Clue

GUARDIAN ANGELS: Every disciple is assisted by a Guru, a Guardian Angel.

Invoke the help of the Master or Guardian Angel before starting the practice of astral projection. Pray, beforehand, to your Inner God so that He may call the Guru in the sacred language.

Undoubtedly, it is viable to that Master to take the disciple consciously out in the Astral Body.

The students that have totally ruined their faculties due to bad habits and customs which they had in past reincarnations are not few in number. This is why they now suffer the unutterable, since in spite of knowing all the Gnostic clues, they do not achieve the conscious projection in the Astral Body.

In the jungles of the Amazon and the Putumayos, a portentous plant named "yague" exists. The Piachis (curanderos) of the tribes take an infusion of that plant mixed with "guarumo" and thus project themselves into the Astral. They take this infusion daily for a certain period of time, thus this is how they acquire the faculty of astralizing themselves. After a while they do not need to drink it anymore; since they no longer need it, because this faculty is endowed permanently within them. However, we do not recommend that Gnostic students, who do not have the faculty of consciously projecting into the Astral, drink that infusion. What we do recommend is practice, much practice and soon they will instantaneously attain conscious astral projection.

Special Clue of "Discernment"

During the hours of sleep, every human being moves in the Astral plane, floating out of the physical body. Even so, unfortunately, during the hours of sleep, within the Internal Worlds human beings wander about with their consciousness absolutely asleep. Generally, they just perform the same daily routine of their life. However, if their consciousness was awaken, instead of dedicating themselves to those nocturnal tasks, they would have the opportunity to contemplate all the marvels of the Superior Worlds with their astral eyes; thus, they would dedicate themselves to study the great mysteries of life and death.

The Theurgist has to acquire a practical,
infallible capacity to consciously
project himself in the Astral Body.

Therefore, here we reveal a clue to awaken astral conscious-ness within the Superior Worlds, precisely during the time of normal sleep.

Exercise: At any given moment during the vigil state, dur-ing the hustle and bustle of daily life, it is necessary to become accustomed to the exercise of "discernment." For example, when a student gazes at the purple color of a beautiful sunset, the most logical question that he should ask himself is: "Am I in the Astral Body? Am I now wandering about out of the physical body?"

There, immediately after those questions, the student must execute a small jump, an upward leap, with the intention of floating. Evidently, if he manages to float it is because he is performing the jump in the Astral Body; his physical body (except all of its vital faculties) was left in his bed sleeping, inactive.

Gnostic disciples must remember and grasp the fact that during sleep, the soul see things in the Astral world exactly as those that exist in the physical world; thus, this is why, every-body during their normal sleep, firmly believes that they are acting in the physical body.

Notwithstanding, the Law of Levitation reigns in the Internal Worlds, while in the physical world the Law of Gravity reigns!

Consequently, the execution of a small jump solves the question: if one floats, it is because one is in the Astral, thus, the Consciousness awakens.

Therefore, every detail, everything that piques our curios-ity, (i.e. every beautiful landscape of Nature) must be worthy of "discernment;" the student must ask the aforementioned ques-tions and thereafter execute the jump.

The following is an illustrative example of the events of daily life. Our friend John, mentioned here many times before, used to do this exercise during his daily life, at every moment, before any detail that piqued his attention or curiosity.

One night John visited some friends, who welcomed him with great affection. Thus, contented, seated among them, he was enjoying the conversation. However, since John was habituated (before any important detail) to ask to himself the aforementioned questions, logically, such a meeting of friends was reason enough in order to question himself:

"Am I in the Astral Body? Am I now wandering about out of the physical body?"

Immediately, he looked around him, and evidently every-thing showed that he was in the physical body. Some of his friends were dressed in trench coats; while some were in suits and yet others were dressed in ordinary urban clothing. So, nothing indicated that John was in the Astral. Nevertheless, he said to himself: "I will execute my little jump!"

He, therefore, excused himself from his buddies and left the room. Thus, outside and with the firm intention of flying, he jumped as high as he could. The outcome was astounding, since he remained floating in the environment! He became perfectly aware that he was within his Astral Body and that his physical body was left resting in the bed!

See, if at that moment John had the initiative of asking such questions to himself, it was due to the fact that he for-mulated such questions to himself at every moment during his daily life. To sum up, this is why such practical questions were absolutely recorded within his subconsciousness. Thus now, during the normal sleep, his subconsciousness automatically impelled him to repeat such practical questions precisely when he was out of his physical body. So, the end result was Astral consciousness.

Sequentially, John went back to the room and said the following to his friends: "Friends of mine let me communicate to you that we, who are reunited here, are in the Astral Body. The fact is that you, friends, went to sleep a few hours ago and right now, your physical bodies are in their beds! Yet, here, all of us are in the Astral Plane."

All my friends touched and looked at each other and said: "That is impossible! We are in the physical body, in flesh and bones!"

They ended up laughing at John. They laughed like madmen. Therefore, when John saw the naiveté of his friends or rather, that they were with their consciousness asleep, he withdrew from the room. While floating in his Astral Body he thought to fly towards San Francisco, California; he wanted to visit a certain temple, which an Initiate founded there, and so he went.

An Unconscious Disincarnated Person

Once on his way, flying in his Astral Body, John glimpsed a man down below, who was traveling by foot. The man was a cargo man, who was carrying a huge load on his back; such a load was very heavy.

When John observed him closely, he could perceive that this person was deceased! He had physically died a short time ago! Yet, now, within his Astral Body, he restlessly walked along that road, convinced that he was within his physical body. He was not conscious of his death; he walked with his consciousness asleep! The load he carried on his strong shoulders was nothing but a mental image created by his mind. This wretched man had physically worked as a cargo man, yet now, after death, he continued on the same job, carrying huge mental loads on his back.

Therefore, with the goal of awakening this man's consciousness, John said the following:

"Friend, be aware of your condition; bear in mind that you are dead; you do not have a physical body anymore."

With somnambulist's eyes the man looked at John, yet he did not understand what John was trying to make him comprehend. Then, by floating around him, John made another attempt. Nevertheless everything was futile! The man had his consciousness asleep, thus any attempt to awaken him was a complete failure.

If this man, during his physical life, when he was in possession of the physical body, would have practiced the clue of "discernment," he would have then been capable of awakening his consciousness during his normal sleep; thus, now after death, he would have become conscious of his disincarnated condition and would have thus become a conscious disciple of the great White Lodge.

Therefore, John gave up any other attempts and continued on his way towards the main purpose of his journey, finally arriving at the temple.

After a while, John happily flew back to his home and returned to his physical body by entering through the pineal gland, which is the window of Brahma, the seat of the soul (as stated by Descartes).

We guarantee the effectiveness of the clue here revealed, since the disciples who have practiced it and attained the awakening of their consciousness within the Internal Worlds are innumerable. What is fundamental is to practice the clue constantly, during the vigil state, since this is the only way for our subconsciousness to register the clue and thus to automatically repeat it during normal sleep.

This practice is one of the ways that the subconsciousness can be placed under the service of conscious will.

Immediately after normal sleep, in the very moment of returning into the physical body (when the consciousness is returning again to the normal vigil state), the student must not physically move in his bed, since with the movement of his physical body, the Astral Body is agitated and the subconscious memories are lost.

So, during those still moments, the students must practice a retrospective exercise in order to remember the places where they traveled, and the things they learned about while acting in their Astral Body.

9: Special Exercises

Clairvoyance (Retrospection)

In the world of occultism, the most known and powerful exercise to develop clairvoyance is the "retrospective exercise."

The disciple begins this exercise as follows: By absorbing himself into a profound internal meditation, he tries to remember in detail the last incidents that happened during that day of his life; then he will penetrate within the memories of the previous day; thereafter into the memories of the day before, and so forth and so on, successively. He must, therefore, apply his retrospective perception and attention to the entire drama of his life. Through the "retrospective exercise," he will recollect the memories of the last fifteen days; then, from the previous month; then, from the month before last... subsequently, the previous year, then, the year before that, etc. as when one is reviewing the contents of a book, from the last page to the first, without skipping any of the pages in between.

The retrospective exercise becomes very difficult when one tries to gain access into the memories of the first seven years of childhood. However, we must acknowledge that all incidents, all representations from that period of our childhood are stored within the "storage of our subconsciousness." Hence, it is imperative to retrieve those memories from the depths of our "storage," out to the light of our consciousness.

This retrieving of our childhood memories is only possible during the moments of falling asleep (since every human being enters into contact with their subconsciousness during normal sleep). Therefore, during those moments of falling asleep, the disciple will combine the retrospective exercise with his drowsiness. Again, the student will make great efforts to retrospectively retrieve from his memory all the incidents of his life until reaching the age of seven. Then, from the seventh year to the first year of life, he will review each year, going further back until the moment of birth. You can be sure that, after arduous efforts and numerous and unwearied retrospective exercises, night after night, little by little, all the memories of childhood will be retrieved.

Reincarnation and Special Mantra

The student can combine the retrospective exercise with the following mantras:

Rrrrraaaaa... Ooooooommmmmmmmmm

These mantras must be chanted as follows:

Raaaaaaaa... Ommmmmmmmmmmmmmmmm. Vocalize these mantras mentally.

Once the student has reviewed his present life, back to his birth, he will then be prepared to make the leap towards the memories related with the last moments of life from his former reincarnation. Naturally, this retrieval of past life's memories implies more effort, as well as a great amount of energy. The student will then combine the retrospective exercise with drowsiness and mantras. He will then retrieve his past (former) life (stored within his memory) by remembering the last moment of that reincarnation, and from there the second to last moment, old age, maturity, youth, adolescence, childhood. Be positive, you will succeed!

During these exercises "astral projection" is normally produced.

The student who has been capable of retrieving the memories of his past reincarnations is acknowledged as a clairvoyant. Thus, from that moment, he will be capable of studying the complete history of the Earth and its races within the memories of Nature.

The retrospective exercise makes the frontal chakra spin.

Special Mantras for Clairaudience

Clairaudience is the sense of hearing with the "occult ear." It is developed with the following mantras:

Jeuse

Vocalization: Jjjjjjjeeeeeee... Uuuuu... Sssss... Eeeee

Vause

Vocalization: Vvvvaaaaa... Uuuuu... Sssss.....Eeeeeee

(As you see, the sound of the above repeated letters must be prolonged).

Absorbed within profound meditation, the student will vocalize while entering into a state of slumber.

Once he succeeds in entering into a state of slumber, he will compel himself to hear the voice of his friends who live far away: this is how "internal hearing" is developed.

Here is another mantra that facilitates the development of clairaudience:

Aum Chiva Tun E

(Note: all vowels are pronounced as short vowel sounds)

Vocalize the mantra AUM as follows: in order to pronounce the "A" open the mouth wide, then round out the mouth as if pronouncing an O and close the lips with the M. Prolong the sound of each vowel.

Vocalize the mantra CHI by prolonging the sound of the vowel "I."

Prolong the "A" of the mantra VA.

When chanting the mantra TUN, pronounce the "T" with force over the "U"; then prolong the U as long as possible and in the end resound the N like a bell-like impacted sound.

Finally, prolong the "E" alone as long as possible, as follows:

Eeeeeeeeeeeeeeeeeee

When chanting the mantra AUM, raise the pitch with the vowel "A" and lower it when chanting "UM." Thereafter, chant the rest of the mantras - CHIVA TUN E - in a lower pitch than UM.

Special Exercise for the Heart Chakra

The heart chakra develops with meditation and the most profound prayer.

We advise you to pray the "Pater Noster."

A well-prayed "Pater Noster" is equivalent to one hour of meditation; pray, therefore, the "Pater Noster" for one hour.

To pray is to converse with God. Hence, immerse yourself into a very profound slumber state and meditate very deeply, thus, converse mentally with God. Each phrase of the "Pater Noster" is a complete formula in order to talk to Him. So, while in a slumber state, meditate on the contents of each phrase, this is how the Father, Who is in secret, can be seen and heard. This is how the heart chakra awakens.

PATER NOSTER

Our Father, who art in heaven, hallowed be Thy name.

Thy kingdom come.

Thy will be done on earth, as it is in heaven.

Give us this day our daily bread,

And forgive us our trespasses, as we forgive those who trespass against us.

And lead us not into temptation, but deliver us from evil.

For thine is the kingdom, the power, and the glory forever.

Amen.

Special Exercise for the Solar Plexus

Remember that the solar plexus is the center of telepathy. Seated in a comfortable chair, the disciple will face the East. Then, he will imagine, far away in that distant east, an immense, radiant and beautiful, golden-colored cross. Imagine that the cross is emitting blue and golden shafts of light, which reach the solar plexus (located at the region of the navel). The disciple will be compelled to feel the vibrations of those shafts of light bathing the chakra of that plexus.

Simultaneously, chant the mantra, which is the vowel U. This vowel must be prolonged for as long as possible, in a semi-deep pitch:

Uuuuuuuuuuuuuuuuuuuuuuuu...

Practice this exercise for half an hour daily. Thus, telepathy will be developed.

When the chakra of the solar plexus is developed, it saturates the frontal chakra with splendor and fire; this is how the clairvoyant chakra perceives all of the luminous colors of the person's aura as well as "the shapes of all thoughts" that float with their glowing colors within the Superior Worlds.

Special Exercise for the Internal Worlds

The following exercise grants the ability to perceive that which exists within the Internal Worlds, within any plane: physical, astral, mental, etc.

When the student needs to clairvoyantly perceive something urgently, he will immerse himself into profound, internal mediation while vocalizing the mantra: ***Proweoa***

Vocalize it by prolonging the sound of each vowel. It is necessary for the esotericist students to learn how to profoundly concentrate.

Profound concentration, perfect meditation, and supreme adoration are the three steps of Initiation.

Concentration, meditation, adoration, and mantras convert us into authentic theurgists.

Concentration, meditation, and supreme adoration lead us to the experience of Samadhi.

We must know how to concentrate.

We must know how to meditate.

We must know how to vocalize the mantras, and we must know how to adore.

Jahve tempts Jesus

Engraving by Gustave Doré

10: Light and Darkness

Esoteric Antithesis

There exist two Lodges that mutually combat each other: the White and the Black, light and darkness!

There, where the light shines, most limpid and intense, likewise the pitch-black darkness coincides with it. Thus, the double of every Angel of light is an Angel of darkness.

Thus, the double of every temple of light is a temple of darkness.

We have already explained the mystery of the twin souls in our *Esoteric Treatise of Theurgy* [page 93].

It is stated that the great Initiate Siddhartha Gautama (Shakyamuni Buddha) had a brother and rival named Devadatta, who, according to Buddhists, represents the king of hell.

Every person has a "human double" incarnated within them. This double is exactly alike in physiognomy, attitudes, manners, in certain capacities, etc. (note that this double is not a reference to the Ethereal Double or the Astral Double). This double is different, it is another type of "personality," it is the antithetic twin soul. Such a soul is the "double." This double possesses the same physical features. It is the exact antithesis of the person.

Likewise, the White Lodge has an antithesis: the Black Lodge. The black magicians of the Black Lodge struggle to swerve initiates off the path. This is why it is necessary, urgent, that the devotees defend themselves from the attacks of the tenebrous ones. Thus, it is urgent to learn how to do so.

Diverse Methods of Attack by the Tenebrous Ones

The tenebrous ones have, at their disposal, infinite resources in order to attack people in different ways:

1. During dreams.

2. During the vigil state.

3. By means of works of black magic.

4. By means of psychic obsessions.

5. By means of enmities

6. By means of organic illnesses.

7. By means of vices.

8. By means of certain aspects of culture.

9. By means of false prophets.

10. By means of the intervention of "inferior elementaries."

Oneiric Seduction by Black Magicians

Those who tread the path are often erotically attacked by the tenebrous ones (usually at night) while their bodies repose during their normal sleep. Temples of black magic exist in the Internal Worlds, thus, naturally, their tenebrous members send certain very beautiful and seductive black sorceresses to male students, with the sole purpose of making them fall sexually.

They know that if the student spills the seminal liquid, the Kundalini descends and thus the weak and naive student loses power.

Mantric Chant

Therefore, it is necessary for the students to learn how to defend themselves from these tenebrous nocturnal erotic attacks. To that effect, the Angel Aroch revealed a mantric chant to us, for personal defense against the tenebrous ones. Sing this mantric chant before going to sleep:

> *Belilin... Belilin... Belilin...*
> *Amphora of salvation.*
> *I would like to be next to you;*
> *Materialism has no power close to me.*
> *Belilin... Belilin... Belilin...*

These mantras must be chanted by placing all our love and sentiment into them. This is how we defend ourselves from the tenebrous ones.

Remember that in the dawning of life, the progenitors of the Gods delightfully sang (and thus taught) the Cosmic Laws to the builders of the Universe.

We must chant these mantras with all of our soul. We must chant them with profound emotion.

This is how we defend ourselves from the tenebrous ones.

When the human being becomes accustomed to practicing Sexual Magic every day, it is then impossible for the tenebrous ones to discharge his valuable seminal reserve; moreover, the nocturnal seminal emissions cease, if there were any at all.

Temptations in the Vigil State

Black magicians usually malevolently employ many people of the opposite sex in order to sexually attack the neighbor. This is "temptation."

Thus, in any sexually tempting, critical situation, the aforementioned mantra also serves to edify an efficient defense against those perverse temptations.

The Vigil State and Bewitchments

Usually, black magicians malevolently and persistently employ their black magic in order to harm their victims. This is why frequently, certain patients with mysterious illnesses (which are the outcome of "bewitchments") need to go to medical clinics. Typically, doctors will prescribe bromides and all kinds of medicines for stress. The sick patients ingest their dosage of medicine, nonetheless they continue going from bad to worse!

The utilization of dolls is one of the most detestable and common methods used by black magicians in order to harm their victims. Of course, we abstain from explaining how these dolls are used or how the tenebrous ones do it, so as not to

provide weapons to certain irresponsible and inhumane individuals.

Symptoms and Theurgic Therapy

It is easily to recognize the symptoms of somebody who
has been assaulted by means of dolls: The person feels a great
anguish, intense palpitations of the heart, depression, pierc-
ing pains in the brain and externally on the temples, pain in
the heart as well as in other areas of the body. In such cases,
healing sessions must be arranged in order to cure these
"bewitched" patients.

To that effect, the patient will be seated in a chair before
a table covered with a white tablecloth. A crucifix, a glass of
water and a lit candle will be placed on the table. The thauma-
turgist (healer) will sit in front of the patient. Other concerned
people, if any, such as friends or relatives of the patient, will
also be seated around the table, under the condition that they
possess a sincere faith of great strength.

Moreover, it is indispensable to place salt and alcohol on a
plate. However, the salt must be previously prepared with the
following exorcism:

Exorcism of Salt

> **In isto sale sit sapientia, et ab omni corruptione servet
> mentes nostras et corpora nostra, per Chokmahel et in
> virtute Ruach-Chokmahel, recedant ab isto fantasmata
> hylae ut sit sal coelestis, sal terrae et terris salis, ut
> nutrietur bos triturans et addat spei nostrae cornua
> tauri volantis. Amen.**

Thereafter, when everything is properly arranged and set,
the great Masters of Light must be invoked by reciting (in a
loud voice) the Invocation of Solomon.

Procedure: Ignite the alcohol with a match so that it burns
with the salt and recite the Invocation of Solomon in that precise moment as follows:

Powers of the kingdom, be ye under my left foot and in my right hand!

Glory and eternity, take me by the two shoulders, and direct me in the paths of victory!

Mercy and justice, be ye the equilibrium and splendor of my life!

Intelligence and wisdom, crown me!

Spirits of Malkuth, lead me betwixt the two pillars upon which rests the whole edifice of the temple!

Angels of Netzach and Hod, establish me upon the cubic stone of Yesod!

Oh Gedulahel! Oh Geburahel! Oh Tiphereth!

Binahel, be thou my love!

Ruach Chokmahel, be thou my light!

Be that which thou art and thou shalt be, Oh Ketheriel!

Ishim, assist me in the name of Shaddai!

Cherubim, be my strength in the name of Adonai!

Beni-Elohim, be my brethren in the name of the Son, and by the powers of Sabaoth!

Elohim, do battle for me in the name of Tetragrammaton!

Malachim, protect me in the name of Iod-Havah!

Seraphim, cleanse my love in the name of Eloah!

Hasmalim, enlighten me with the splendors of Elohim and Shechinah!

Aralim, act!

Ophanim, revolve and shine!

Chaioth-Ha-Kadosh cry, speak, roar, bellow!

Kadosh, Kadosh, Kadosh!

Shaddai, Adonai, Iod-Havah, Eheieh asher Eheieh!

Hallelu-Jah, Hallelu-Jah, Hallelu-Jah.

Amen. Amen. Amen.

After having recited this invocation with fervor and with intense faith, we will beg the great Masters of the Light to heal the patient.

Sequentially, the theurgist will recite (filled with all of his spiritual strength of profound faith, and with confidence in his power), the following conjuration:

CONJURATION OF THE SEVEN OF SOLOMON THE SAGE

In the name of Michael, may Jehovah command thee and drive thee hence, Chavajoth!

In the name of Gabriel, may Adonai command thee, and drive thee hence, Bael!

In the name of Raphael, begone before Elial, Samgabiel!

By Samael Sabaoth, and in the name of Elohim Gibor, get thee hence, Andrameleck!

By Zachariel et Sachiel-Meleck, be obedient unto Elvah, Sanagabril!

By the divine and human name of Shaddai, and by the sign of the Pentagram which I hold in my right hand, in the name of the angel Anael, by the power of Adam and Eve, who are Iod-Chavah, begone Lilith! Let us rest in Peace, Nahemah!

By the holy Elohim and by the names of the Genii Cashiel, Sehaltiel, Aphiel and Zarahiel, at the command of Orifiel, depart from us Moloch! We deny thee our children to devour!

Amen. Amen. Amen.

Destruction of Malignant Fluids and Larvae by Means of Fire

Notice, it is also necessary to have next to the patient, a brazier (a metal pan for holding burning coals or charcoal, such as a hibachi), filled with charcoal that must be lit and left to get red-hot. Thus, with his right hand the theurgist will perform fast and energetic magnetic passes over the sick organs, and he will immediately cast the harmful, deleterious (magnetic) fluids (that have been removed from the victim) onto the burning charcoals.

Once the ceremony has ended, the patient must drink the glass of water that was on the table, since the Masters of the Light have already placed their sacred medicine within that water.

Saint Thomas stated that the concoction of sage and rue plants must be drunk to ward off spells; we should also smudge ourselves with them.

The procedure that we have revealed and taught here in order to heal the sick (who have been harmed by sorcery through dolls) can also be employed successfully to combat any type of bewitchment.

Black Elementals, Bats

We must warn students that not only do sorcerers use "dolls" in order to make their victims ill, but also the "elementals" of some animals. This is why witches or sorcerers possess millions of methods and influences in order to impiously cause all kinds of harm to their victims.

Unluckily, we met a black magician who sent vampires or bats to the homes of his hated victims with the intention of causing them fatal harm. Through his ominous "works" of black magic, by manipulating his armies of repugnant chiropters with malignant ability, this tenebrous man became wealthy. He nourished these innocent animals with plantain oils; nonetheless, when these elementals resisted in obeying him, he then punished them by denying them any type of food. We will obviously not explain the procedures of that sorcerer, because we do not teach black magic.

How to Surprisingly Trap Sorceresses

Obviously, there exist sorceresses as well as sorcerers. These women possess secrets (i.e. as those which we have revealed in this book) in order to submerge their physical bodies within the fourth dimension. This is how they immerse their physical bodies within the tenebrous regions of Nature and travel to remote places in order to cause hideous damages to people. Nevertheless, it is easy to trap them.

THE METHOD: On the floor, place a pair of scissors opened in the form of a cross, and scatter black mustard seed inside the room of the victim. This procedure will cause the witches to fall!

An Objective Testimony

We knew the case of a lady who did not believe in witches. She had the same mental conditioning as numerous other people have; she was intellectualized with concepts acquired through conventional culture.

Well then, the aforementioned woman visited a female cousin, who lived in the city.

In the evening, the two women saw a blackish bird, which looked like a buzzard or a vulture. This bird was perched on a tree in the outdoor patio of the house and from the tree the bird was mimicking the words that the two women were saying in their conversation and thereafter laughing at them.

That night, the cousin, who comprehended what this bird of evil omen was, placed a pair of scissors on the floor in the form of a cross and scattered black mustard seed inside of her bedroom.

The outcome was astounding: that evil omen bird, that was still perched on the tree in the outdoor patio, entered the bedroom of the house, flapped incessantly and then fell down upon the scissors! Thereafter, before the shocking eyes of her cousin, the bird inevitably was transformed into a woman. The woman was completely naked. Thus, the angry and inflexible cousin lashed the witch horribly with a whip and thereafter threw her out naked into the street. After a while some neighbors, feeling pity for the witch, gave her some clothes to cover up her body. This is a factual historical case.

Maculae Produced through Bewitchments

The wretched and suffering victims of bewitchments have their skin covered with huge black spots. Generally, the doctors of medicine do not ever manage to discover and understand .the origin of these mysteriously colored maculae on the skin.

Nevertheless, these spots on the skin can also be healed (made to disappear) by means of the former liturgical ritual that was taught in this chapter. Nonetheless, we must warn that a single healing session is not enough in order to succeed. Any illness produced by bewitchment can be healed in exactly six months with constant, tenacious and persistent daily work.

When it is suspected that the victim has ingested some malignant substance, then, one spoonful of olive oil must be drunk daily on an empty stomach; one hour later (after drinking the olive oil), the person must drink the concoction of "epazote macho," which is also called "yerba santa" or "paico."

Saint Ignatius' Fava Bean and "Yellow Water"

However, in very serious and desperate cases, the patient will be purged by consuming Saint Ignatius' Fava Bean (which is a very drastic almond) on an empty stomach. Saint Ignatius' Fava Bean will make the victims of the black magicians vomit the malignant substances from their stomach.

Likewise, in these cases, a cleansing of the stomach can be performed with what is called "Yellow Water." This water is prepared in the following manner: Fill a one liter yellow colored bottle (or various bottles of the same yellow color) with water. Mix one gram of yellow vegetable aniline (food dye) in the water of each bottle (the aniline is the one utilized to dye candies or in the baking industry to make bread appear yellow. Do not ever use a mineral aniline or colorant).

Close the bottles and place them under the rays of the Sun for two hours. Thereafter, every hour, give the patient (who has been harmed with malignant substances) a glassful of this "Yellow Water" to drink. Continue the treatment constantly for as long as necessary.

"Funerary" Substances

There are patients who have been harmed without any scruples, without even the most basic scruples; they were harmed with funerary substances or with other types of suspicious substances, yet not less repugnant.

Likewise, these cases can be healed with the "Yellow Water."

The person that became sick because of the ingestion of funerary substances, presents the following symptoms: a cadaverous color; if he is average (not too fat nor too thin) he becomes spectral, extremely skeletal and feeble, to the point that his bones are easily exposed; moreover, he feels a constantly moving, turning ball inside of his stomach.

A patient like this can be healed with the rite already described in this chapter, and with "Yellow Water."

Children who have been perversely harmed with funerary substances also exist. However, in some of these cases the people who have caused the harm did it unintentionally and unconsciously. For example, we know of the case of a girl who was about two years old, whose physical appearance was exactly like that of a specter. This happened because her relatives had attended a burial or funeral in the cemetery. Thus, upon returning home from the burial ground, they made contact with the girl, and naturally, they touched her. Thus, in this way they contaminated her with deadly and infectious, bodiless vital fluids.

Physicians failed totally in this case. Yet, we, the brethren of the temple, prescribed for her nine healing baths of milk with peppermint. This bath is easily prepared: the peppermint plant is boiled with the milk, thereafter, bathe the sick child with it. These nine baths are taken for nine consecutive days. The outcome was excellent: the little girl was totally healed.

The Evil Eye

It seems incredible, yet the fact is that there exist people who have a terribly hypnotic force; when they look at a child, sometimes the child inevitably dies.

SYMPTOMS: Great black circles under the eyes; fever in the head; vomiting and diarrhea.

In these cases the theurgist will execute magnetic passes over the whole body of the child, especially on the head and on the face. In this manner, he will imagine that he is removing the harmful fluids with energy; he will then immediately cast these (magnetic) fluids onto the hot embers of very well lit charcoal.

The energetic passes over the whole body are performed simultaneously with the recitation of the Conjuration of the Seven of the Wise King Solomon.

In most cases, thousands of children die in the cities due to this inflicted harm. The physicians who give the children death certificates usually affirm that these children have died because of an intestinal infection. A great number of children could be saved in the cities if their parents would utilize healing methods that can cure them; the parents should not worry about people's open criticism.

The "evil eye" can be prevented by adorning the children with small gold rings placed on their small fingers or by making bracelets of genuine coral for them to wear. The jet mineral can also be used.

Magical Circle

The magical circle is utilized as a defense against the attacks of the tenebrous ones. This circle must not be completely closed since this drawn circle must be interrupted by the Seal of Solomon.

This seal is integrated by the two antagonistic ternaries: the ternary of the light and the ternary of the darkness.

The first is the Internal Christ of every human being: the resplendent Dragon of Wisdom: Father, Son, and Holy Spirit.

The second is the three-headed Black Dragon: the "psychological I," which is composed of the three traitors that assassinated Hiram Abiff, who in turn is the Master, the superior ternary of the human being, his Inner God.

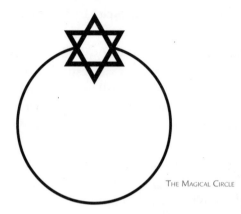

THE MAGICAL CIRCLE

The Black Dragon is triune: it controls the Astral, Mental and Causal Bodies. This is the Medusa whose head is lodged with poisonous serpents.

Know well that every human being must decapitate Medusa with the flaming sword of Perseus.

Therefore, the disciples who want to defend themselves against the attacks of black magic must habituate themselves to mentally trace the magical circle.

The magical circle can be performed before falling into normal sleep or whenever it is necessary.

(Excerpt from *Occult Medicine and Practical Magic:* When you trace a Magical Circle around yourself, whether it be with your sword, or with your willpower and Imagination united in vibrating harmony (or with both at the same time), you must pronounce the following mantras: ***Helion, Melion, Tetragrammaton.***)

11: White Magic and Black Magic

Obsessed and Possessed

Black magicians can also make their victims become obsessed with fixed ideas. Likewise, numerous cases of being possessed exist within the Gospels.

Generally, mediums of spiritualism become obsessed by "larvae" and by demons that populate the lower regions of the Astral World.

All these cases are cured by reciting the Conjuration of the Four in front of the manic person, as follows:

CONJURATION OF THE FOUR

Caput mortum, imperet tibi dominus per vivum et devotum serpentem!

Cherub, imperet tibi Dominus per Adam Iod-Havah!

Aquila errans, imperet tibi Dominus per alas tauri!

Serpens, imperet tibi Dominus Tetragrammaton, per Angelum et Leonem!

Michael, Gabriel, Raphael, Anael!

Fluat udor per Spiritum Elohim

Manet in terra per Adam Iod-Chavah!

Fiat firmamentum per Iod-Havah -Sabaoth!

Fiat judicium per ignem in virtute Michael!

Angel of the blind eyes, obey, or pass away with this holy water!

Work winged bull, or revert to the earth, unless thou wilt that I should pierce thee with this sword!

Chained eagle, obey my sign, or fly before this breathing!

Writhing serpent, crawl at my feet, or be tortured by the sacred fire and give way before the perfumes that I burn in it!

Water, return to water!

Fire, burn!

Air, circulate!

Earth, revert to earth!

By virtue of the Pentagram, which is the morning star, and by the name of the Tetragram, which is written in the center of the cross of Light!

Amen. Amen. Amen.

RITUAL: The Conjuration of the Seven of the King Solomon can also be recited. Its meaning is already explained in our book *Esoteric Treatise of Theurgy.*

Moreover, perform smudges with sage and rue on the sick person; to that effect the plants must be burned over lit, red-hot charcoals and by following the procedures already described in the former chapter.

The Pentagram of Solomon must be traced on the floor of the threshold (entrance) of the door, just as it is shown in the following illustration:

THE PENTAGRAM

The superior angle of the star of five points will be directed towards the interior of the room; the two opposing angles must face the outside of the room. This must be traced on the floor with charcoal.

Thereafter, the tenebrous ones will be commanded, "***In the name of Christ, by the power of Christ, by the majesty of Christ***" to abandon the body of the victim.

Enmities

Black magicians manipulate people in order to make them the enemies of other people. Thus, the enemies fueled by the Black Lodge attack the victims.

Hence, if students do not know how control themselves or restrain themselves or overcome themselves, they fail and withdraw from the path.

Disciples must control enemies, dissolve enmities with the following clue:

Lie down on the bed. Relax all the muscles of the body. Enter into a slumber state and concentrate on the heart of the enemy. Imagine the enemy's heart like a tabernacle that treasures infinite love. Then, mentally place your image (the image of the disciple, an image full of love) within the enemy's heart.

Subsequently, the disciple must imagine that he is looking at the area between the enemy's eyebrows. Thereafter, the disciple must place his/her image, full of intense love, between the two eyebrows of the enemy, within the enemy's mind. In this exercise, it is necessary for the disciple to feel a true love for that enemy that hates him.

Let us understand that this is not a matter of trying to pretend we love the enemy: for us, it is indispensable for the feeling of love to surge forth towards that individual, towards the enemy who hates us. However, if, despite all of this, the enemy persists in causing us harm, then we must work with the maguey.

The Elemental of the Maguey (Agave Americana)

If the student lives in an urban setting, then, he must travel to the outskirts of the city or to a hamlet and search for a maguey in the countryside. There, with a small stick he will trace on the ground (from right to left), a circle around the maguey. The dimensions of the circle around the plant should be about eight hand spans. Afterwards, the student must bless the maguey and beg the "elemental" of the plant to depart to wherever the enemy (whose action the student is trying to counteract) is located, and to disintegrate the enemy's evil thoughts. Then with a sharp knife, cut a piece of the leaf of the maguey. The piece of the cut leaf must be placed between the palms of the hands, then, command

the "elemental" of the maguey with imperative will to exert supreme obedience to us. The elemental must be commanded to immediately leave and be near the enemy and to stay close to him in order to disintegrate his evil thoughts. Simultaneously the required mantras must be pronounced.

The mantras that must be pronounced in the moments when practicing this entire ritual are as follows:

Libib Lenoninas Lenonon

Unto each letter of the mantra, provide a bell-like impact of resonance. The outcome will be astounding. This is how the elemental of the maguey will disintegrate the wicked self-willed thoughts and feelings of hate of the enemy, thus, in the end, the enemy will become a friend.

Understand that in these exercises, what is essential is to truly and with all our heart love those who declare themselves to be our enemy.

Likewise, in urgent and grave cases, the disciples can defend themselves from their enemies with these other following mantras:

Klim Krishnaya, Govindaya, Gopijana, Vallabhaya, Swaha.

Vices and Bad Habits

Often, the tenebrous ones take advantage of people's tendency towards vices (i.e. use of liquors, drugs, the vice of fornication, etc.). They do this in order to deviate them from the path and in order to inflict severe harm on them.

Every disciple or Master of the White Lodge must abstain from all of this.

Regarding social gatherings: those initiates who have strong will, sometimes politely allow themselves to sip or to taste up to three small quantities of liquor or up to three small quantities of beer. They never go beyond three; if they do, they violate the law.

Subliminal images and exploits of black magic are abundant within the atmosphere of theaters, since the Black Lodge has them under its control. For instance, spectators contemplate actors performing pornographic scenes or listen to words with double or malevolent meaning. These tenebrous elements of depraved enjoyment hurt the retina and the ear and even penetrate the mind. Then, in the Mental Plane, the psychological "I" of every person intervenes by creating mental living effigies that become absolute replicas of the stage images, which captivated the retina and the ear of the spectator. These effigies are endowed with consciousness and become true "mental demons" which (during the hours of normal sleep) fornicate several times with the spectator's mind. Obviously, this causes nocturnal pollutions (wet dreams).

Cinemas are worse because within them these depraved elements are more abundant due to the extremely noxious popularity that film makers have impressed on their movies. Disciples should abstain from going to movie theaters.

Unfortunately, in this day and age, theaters and cinemas with their undercover corruption or evident practices of black magic are centers (because of their audacity towards perversion) that have been transformed into explicit and unmistakable temples of black magic, which are unhealthy to the mental state of people.

Even worse conclusions or allegations (yet precise and woeful) can be aimed at night clubs which have inflicted so much evil onto the morality of today's youth.

Therefore, disciples should know how to defend themselves from the above mentioned filthy temptations.

Moreover, there are women who unknowingly accumulate great amounts of Luciferic force. Often these women are not necessarily that beautiful; yet they fall under the service of the Luciferic force. This is why naive male disciples become irresistibly tempted by them; the disciples fight against the temptation, yet the weak end up falling into these women's atmospheres and fail on their path by fatally submitting themselves to these temptations. Indeed, these women with their Luciferic force hypnotize and attract the weak.

Nevertheless, a sacred clue to defend ourselves from these terrible temptations exists: this is the "Pater Noster." Hence, the Prayer of the Lord fervently prayed and meditated on without haste and with a great amount of willpower is the clue.

Negative Action of Culture

The tenebrous ones are terribly intellectual. We have known black magicians brilliantly talented with sharp intellects. These tenebrous ones manipulate the intellects of esoteric students and use the intellect as an instrument in order to swerve the students from the Royal Path of Light. These Luciferic tenebrous ones, besides being extraordinarily intellectual, are also perverse fornicators.

Many aspects of the present modern culture or militant culture reveal the intervention or influence of these intellectualizing tenebrous ones.

Esoteric students must defend themselves from all of these unhealthy and dastardly intellectualisms (as any explorer of the Paths of Light or as any aspirant to the Superior Worlds would do) by listening to the voice of their own heart, by listening to the voice of their own zeal and of their own inner Divinity, their inner God.

False Prophets

Any false prophet is a fornicator.

Therefore, any prophet that advises the ejaculation of the seminal liquor is a false prophet who is under the commands of the tenebrous ones of the Black Lodge.

Ye shall know them by their fruits. - Matthew 7:16

Intervention of "Elementaries"

"Elementaries" often harm people, who then become their victims. Various types of "elementaries" exist, namely: kaballis, phantasmata, incubi, succubi, dragons, basilisk, aspis, leos, etc., (read *The Elementals* by Franz Hartmann).

Women who masturbate engender incubi from their spilled seminal fluid.

Likewise, men who masturbate engender succubi from their ejaculated semen.

Incubi are masculine and the succubi are feminine. These "elementaries" incite their progenitors to repeat the perverted vice that gave them life; they live at the expense of the Vital Body of their progenitors. This is how incubi and succubi physically weaken their victims. Asafetida smudges disintegrate the incubi and succubi.

The asafetida plant must be tossed onto lit, red-hot embers and thereafter the smoke will cleanse the environment of larvae; asafetida smudges disintegrates them.

We also recommend spreading sulfur inside the shoes since the ethereal vapors that rise from sulfur disintegrate these dangerous larvae.

The phantasmata elementaries wander around at night and go to the beds of fornicators in order to fecundate their spilled seminal fluid, from which countless larvae of all types emerge. Sulfur and asafetida finish off all these larvae.

A great deal of larvae called dragon invades the bedrooms of prostitutes. This larva is fashioned by spilled seminal fluid, yet it is disintegrated with sulfur and asafetida.

So, "elementaries" make disciples fall into the abyss of temptation. This is why every disciple should use sulfur and asafetida, because black magicians utilize all of these larvae in order to harm and swerve the devotees from the path.

12: The Flaming Forge of Vulcan

The Holy Eight

We have already stated in our book *The Major Mysteries* that humans left Eden through the door of sex and that only through the same door can the return to Eden be achieved. Eden is sex itself!

Max Heindel states that the sign of the infinite, the Holy Eight is found within the heart of the Earth. The great illuminated Master Hilarion IX also affirms this.

Let us explain.

The sign of the infinite is a key to powers. Symbolically, the brain, heart and sex of the planetary genie are placed in it.

Now, if we graphically embody the Holy Eight, then the two circles that form it would represent the sex and the brain respectively, and the center of the eight (where the two circles joint) would symbolize the heart.

The struggle that develops in the destiny of a human is terrible: this is brain against sex and sex against brain..! And what is even more frightening and painful is heart against heart! This is understood by those who have loved a lot...

The Holy Eight and the Caduceus of Mercury

From another point of view, the Holy Eight forms the Caduceus of Mercury, represented by the two already mentioned ganglionic cords that in the Orient are called Ida and Pingala (which are entwined around the spinal medulla).

It has already been stated that the fire rises through one cord and the water through the other cord. These are the fire of Phlegethon and the water of Acheron that cross in the Ninth Sphere forming the sign of the infinite.

The Beheading of Medusa

The Holy Eight and the Frontal Chakra

The great Master, Knight of the Holy Grail, Prince of Jerusalem and Guardian of the Temple, Hilarion IX, stated that by repetitively tracing the sign of the infinite fixed on the frontal chakra and meditating on the Sacred Order of Tibet, the esotericist student will consciously "project" himself or will be projected in his Astral Body into the Astral Plane. Thus, eventually, the student will consciously present himself at the temple of the Sacred Order of Tibet, and after being submitted to numerous ordeals, the magnificent "Arcanum A.Z.F." is delivered from "mouth to ear" to him.

(F + A = C)

F + A = C, means: fire plus aqua (water) is equal to consciousness. Indeed, the fire and the water of the Ninth Sphere (Sex), as instruments of sanctification, have the power to awaken the student's consciousness within the Internal Worlds.

This is how we comprehend the reason why the two witnesses of Revelation give the power of prophecy. (Revelation 11:3)

The Forge of Vulcan

The flaming forge of Vulcan is found in the Ninth Sphere. This forge is sex! Mars descends into the Ninth Sphere in order to re-temper his sword and to conquer the heart of Venus (the Venustic Initiation); Hercules descends also in order to clean the Augean stables (the stables of the Soul) with the sacred fire; and Perseus in order to cut the head of Medusa (Satan, the psychological "I") with the flaming sword.

The esotericist student has to deliver the head of Medusa (lodged with serpents) to Minerva, the Goddess of Wisdom.

The Venustic Initiation can only be conquered in the flaming forge of Vulcan!

Absolute purification can only be achieved in the flaming forge of Vulcan!

The psychological "I", the "myself," which is the Satan mentioned in the sacred Bible, can only be decapitated in the flaming forge of Vulcan.

Whosoever wants to enter into the sacred city of nine doors (that is mentioned in the *Bhagavad-Gita*) must be resolved to descend to the flaming forge of Vulcan.

Narrow is the Door

A great amount of esotericist students mistakenly affirm that there are numerous paths to attain the union with God. However, the divine, great Master Jesus stated: "Strait is the gate, and narrow is the way, which leads unto life, and few there be that find it." (Matthew 7:14)

If esotericist students patiently search everything that is written in the four Gospels, they will then be able to verify that Jesus never stated that there are many paths... The adorable Savior of the World only spoke about one strait gate and one narrow and difficult path..! That gate is sex! And that path is sex..! Another path to attain the union with God does not exist. Throughout eternity, there has never been a prophet that has known another door other than sex..!

Sexual Magic, Not Celibacy

The transmutation of lead into gold is achieved in the flaming forge of Vulcan. The Child of Gold of Alchemy is born in this forge! This marvelous Child is the Son of Man, the Sun-King, the Sun-Man.

Some esotericist students who are mistaken, confused, and who err, reject these teachings and affirm that Pythagoras, Zoroaster, Jesus and other Initiates were celibate and that they never had a spouse, ignoring that sacred vestals existed within all the temples of mysteries. Yet, deplorably the materialists, the disrespectful, the ill-intentioned ignoramuses have arbitrarily labeled them sacred prostitutes. Notwithstanding, these vestals were true initiate virgins. Esoterically, they were virgins, even when their bodies were no longer in the physiological state of virginity.

High Initiates and the Arcanum A.Z.F.

Indeed, the Pythagorean, Zoroastrian, Jesus Christian Initiates and all those ancient Initiates of the temple, without exception, practiced the "Arcanum A.Z.F." with the vestals of the temple... All of them had to descend into the flaming forge of Vulcan in order to cut off the head of Medusa with the flaming sword of Perseus! All of them descended into that flaming forge in order to clean the stables of their Soul and thus obtain the incarnation of the Word in the sacred manger of the consciousness.

Only in that flaming forge could those great initiates re-temper their weapons and conquer the heart of Venus!

The Great Work of the Sun

Those who suppose that there are multiple paths in order to attain the union with God, are totally ignoring that water and oil are necessary in the great work of the Sun: half water... half oil..!

The golden oil which is emptied out through the two golden pipes from the two olive branches of the two olive trees upon the right and upon the left side of the candlestick of the temple is transmuted creative energy. (Zechariah 4:11, 12)

These olive trees, like two children of oil, are born in the sacred lake, in the lake of Genezareth. The sacred lake of Genezareth symbolizes the seminal vesicles where the pure water (fluid) of life is contained...

Whosoever drinks from this pure water of life shall never thirst! Nevertheless, strait is the gate and narrow is the way that leads to Light!

This is why I tell you: strive, brethren of my soul, to enter into the strait and difficult gate, because, truly I say unto you: many will seek to enter in, and shall not be able..!

Woe to the dwellers of the Earth!

Woe to those who do not descend into the flaming forge of Vulcan!

Woe to those who despise the Ninth Sphere!

Woe to those who are scared to enter in at the Ninth Gate!

Woe to those who reject the pure water of life and the sacred oil of the temple!

It would have been better for them to have never been born or for a millstone to be hung about their neck, and drowned in the depths of the sea.

Those will be the lost ones: the failures of the present Fifth Root Race!

The vestals of the temple had a marvelous priestess-hood preparation. Upon them rests the principle which states that the Word is always the child of immaculate conceptions.

The Word is always the child of divine virgins!

The Maximum Ordeal

The descent into the Ninth Sphere was, in ancient mysteries, the highest trial in order to acquire the supreme dignity of the Hierophant

Buddha, Hermes, Rama, Zoroaster, Krishna, Jesus, and Moses had to descend into the Ninth Sphere in order to work with fire and water, origin of worlds, beasts, humans and Gods. Every authentic White Initiation begins here, in the Ninth Sphere, sex.

The human being, in his fetal state, remains for nine months within the maternal womb. Humanity was also within the maternal womb of Nature (namely: Rea, Cibeles, Isis, etc.) for nine ages. Now we comprehend why we call sex the region of the Ninth Sphere. Therefore, the flaming forge of Vulcan is (in its deep significance) the Ninth Sphere.

13: Akasha

The Akasha is Sound; it is the Word

The present book has reached its goal. The objective of this book is to learn how to speak the Verb of Gold, since the mission of every human being is to educate themselves on how to play the lyre of Orpheus. This magnificent lyre is the creative larynx! The mission of every human being is to incarnate the Word!

The Earth is only a condensation of the Word! Everything emerges from the Ether and everything returns to the Ether. Beyond the Ether is the Akasha; this blue, spiritual, and profound, divine essence fills and penetrates the entire infinite space. The Ether turns out to be only the condensation of the pure Akasha.

The Hindu *Puranas* are correct when affirming that sound is an attribute of Akasha.

Indeed, sound blares from within the Logos. Thus, the Akasha becomes the fundamental agent of every theurgic operation.

The Akasha is the Anima Mundi; it is the same as the Kundalini. One of the responsibilities of life is to awake in us, by means of Sexual Magic, that Anima Mundi, that Kundalini, which is a coiled up serpent. Only by its awakening can the great Verb of Gold be heard.

All existences spring forth from the Akasha. The Akasavani is the Voice from the Sky; it is the Word that blares from the Logos! The word of the Logos becomes concrete by means of Akasha.

The Akasha and the Tattvas

The Vayu-Pranas are the sounding waves of pure Akasha.

Thus, when Akasha condenses into Ether, these Vayu-Pranas are transformed into Tejas (Fire), Vayu (Air), Apas

(Water), and Prithvi (Earth). These are the Tattvas that Rama Prasad thoroughly studied.

The Igneous Ether vibrates within every flame; the Gaseous Ether vibrates within the Air; the Liquid Ether vibrates within the Water and the Petrous Ether vibrates within the Earth. These are the Tattvas; the substrates of all of these Tattvas are the Vayu-Pranas, the sounding waves, the Verb, the Great Word.

Prior to the condensation of our planetary globe with its four elements, Fire, Air, Water and Earth, the planetary globe existed in an ethereal state with all of its elements. When these ethereal Tattvas condense, the ethereal elements are then transformed into physicochemical elements.

Indeed, Akasha is the condensation of sound. This Akasha Tattva is the spiritual substance that emanates from Anupadaka (this word means "without parents," "the One existing by itself"). The radical element of matter is found above Akasha.

Beyond Anupadaka is Adhi and beyond Adhi is the Ain Soph (the super divine Atom of the human being).

The Mantra "Invia"

The Creative Logos expresses itself as the Word, as sound. A language of gold exists, humans should utter this language. Before humans were exiled from the "Jinn" Paradises, only the Verb of Gold was spoken, this great universal language has perfect grammar.

When the great Hierophants of ancient Egypt wanted to visit the "Garden of Delights" they grasped with their right hand a legume which is commonly known by the name "deer's eye." They then submerged themselves into profound meditation while pronouncing the mantra **Invia**.

This mantra works as an invocation: when vocalizing it, the elemental of this legume arrives under the irresistible influence of the chanted mantra. The elemental of this legume has the power of placing the body in the "Jinn" state.

When those Hierophants felt that their body began to inflate or swell from the feet up, they then comprehended that their body had acquired the "Jinn" state. Then, filled with faith, they rose from their beds, and were definitely submerged within the "Garden of Delights." Thus, this is how they travelled to different places of the Earth.

Whosoever wants to put into practice the process disclosed above, then, get into a slumber state while meditating on the elemental of the legume "deer's eye."

We inform the esotericist students that a great "Jinn" Master, exists whose name is Oguara. This Master invariably attends the call of those who invoke him. He helps them to submerge their physical body within the fourth dimension.

"Jinn" State Universal Language

In "Jinn Paradises" one employs the great universal language of life in order to speak.

For example, if one wants to say: "I am here fulfilling my mission with great sacrifice," then the former phrase would be uttered by pronouncing the following mantras of the great language of Light:

Lutener Masleim Aeodon

If one wants to utter: "I will be here with you for a little while longer," in the language of gold this phrase would be uttered with the following words:

Masleim Urim Seidau

These are a few phrases of the universal language, which all the inhabitants of Eden speak. This is the language which the divine humanity uttered in times of yore, until the moment when it was cast out from the "Garden of Delights."

Another example: "the Passion of our Lord Jesus Christ," would be described with the following words:

Tiana Pana

Our Gnostic sanctuaries, in the language of gold, would be named with the following words:

Lumicalesc Gnostico

Regarding spiritual development, the initiates who walk on the Fourth Path (the world of the mind), must be aware that the "password" which will allow them to enter into the temples of the Mental Plane is:

Adacripto

The cardinal numbers, one, two, three are named with the following words: **Eba, Doba, Dusna**. The entire priesthood of theurgy is based on these three principles from the resplendent Dragon of Wisdom.

Immodest Action

The clue of all powers and the key of all the empires has been delivered in this book.

In it has been demonstrated that the Akasha is sound.

That the Kundalini is Akasha.

That the Kundalini is sound.

That in order to speak the language of gold the awakening of the Kundalini is necessary, because the Kundalini is the concretion of the Word in each human being.

Therefore, since the Kundalini is sexual, only through Sexual Magic can the awakening of the Kundalini be performed, in order to speak the language of the Light.

In the sacred language of the Light, "immodest action" is uttered with the following words:

Gole Goletero

So, esotericist disciples must abstain from all "immodest action." They must work with the "Arcanum A.Z.F.," (Sexual Magic) at their home only with their priestess-spouse. Those who practice the "Arcanum A.Z.F." with different women violate the Law; they are "immodest," they are adulterers!

It is better to be humble, pure, chaste, and simple. Besides, it is worth more to love our worst enemies, to kiss the feet of those who hate us, to kiss the hand that slaps us, to caress the whip that lashes our flesh. It is more elevated to love those who hate us, indeed, because they do not comprehend us, and to love even more those who love us; to return good for evil and to give our last drop of blood for this wretched suffering humanity.

As well, it is better to learn the language of light, which is recommended in this book; and likewise the language of power, which are the mantras that are written within it.

Why does the human being feel incompetent to learn the divine musical expression of the light, yet for his own (degenerated) slang he feels no scorn? This sinks him into the abysses of evil.

Let us quote some related passages:

Master? Christ!

> *My brethren, be not many masters, knowing that we shall receive the greater condemnation.* - James 3:1

(There is only one Master of Masters, namely Christ, the Perfect Multiple Unity. Nevertheless, whosoever incarnates Christ is a true Master).

Words of Love

> *For in many things we offend all. If anyone offend not in word, the same is a perfect man, and able also to bridle the whole body.* - James 3:2

The words of the student must be filled with infinite love, with infinite sweetness, with infinite harmony and infinite peace because arrhythmic words (although not being vulgar) are also offensive and destructive. Every word charged with anger, every ironic word is a murderous dagger that wounds our neighbor's consciousness in the world of the mind.

To Govern the Tongue

> *Behold we put bits into the horses' mouths that they*
> *may obey us; and we turn about their whole body.* -
> James 3:3

Whosoever attempts to spiritually elevate themselves or whose only aspiration is to learn how to consciously project in their Astral Body, or who yearns for the capacity of traveling in the Mental Body, or who chooses to learn how to consciously move within the World of the Pure Spirit, must govern their tongue.

Only Our Own Internal Satan Glorifies Himself

> *Behold also the ships, which though they be so great,*
> *and are driven of fierce winds, yet are they turned*
> *about with a very small helm, whithersoever the*
> *governor listed.*
>
> *Even so the tongue is a little member, and boasts*
> *great things. Behold, how great a matter a little fire*
> *kindleth!* - James 3:4-5

Whosoever says: "I am a great Master, I am a great Initiate, I possess great powers, I am the reincarnation of such Genie or such hero (even when he might really be)," must know that when he boasts about being all these things, the one who is being glorified through him is the prince of this world, his own particular Satan. Indeed, down here no one has anything worthy of praise or anything to feel proud about or to be vain about, because as humans we are miserable sinners, dirt, dust of the earth. Moreover, up there in heaven, our Being is only a super-divine atom of the Abstract Absolute Space.

The Tongue of the Fornicator

> *And the tongue is a fire, a world of iniquity, so is the*
> *tongue among our members, that it defiles the whole*
> *body, and sets on fire the course of nature; and it is set*
> *on fire of hell.* - James 3:6

Brethren, disciples, esotericist students: the tongue is a fire, a world of iniquity... The Aztecs have in the Temple of Chapultepec (which is in "Jinn" state) a sculpture that represents Tonatiuh with his triangular tongue and his erected phallus. Hence, the inner relationship that exists between the Word and Sexual Magic is perceived in this figure.

When the person is a fornicator, his tongue speaks evilness. Defamation, denigration, and slander are the offspring of a sinful tongue...

No one has the right to judge anyone. No one has the right to condemn anyone! And no one is more worthy than anyone else!

To Dominate Nature

> *For every kind of beasts, and of birds, and of serpents, and of things of the sea, is tamed, and hath been tamed of mankind.* - James 3:7

Indeed, the human being can command and govern Nature with the Verb, with the Word.

For example, poisonous serpents are driven away with the following mantras:

Osi Osoa Asi

Vicious dogs are frightened away with the mantras: **Sua**.

Also with the mantra: **Pas**!

Donkeys are controlled with the vowel "**O**."

We control pigs by repeating the word **Chin** several times.

In the times of draught, the Arhuacos Indians (from La Sierra Nevada of Santa Marta, Colombia) meet in groups and imitate the croaking of frogs. This is how the rain (that they need for their agriculture) falls.

The Tongue Blesses and Curses

> *But the tongue can no man tame; it is an unruly evil, full of deadly poison.*

Therewith we bless God, even the Father; and therewith we curse men, which are made in the image of God.

Out of the same mouth proceeds blessing and cursing; my brethren, these things ought not so to be.

Doth a fountain send forth at the same place sweet water and bitter?

Can the fig tree, my brethren, bear olive berries, either a vine, figs? So a fountain can not yield both salty water and fresh. - James 3:8-12

The brethren of the path must know that no fountain can simultaneously yield both salty water and fresh. Thus, the path cannot be tread while simultaneously speaking sweet and bitter words. We cannot simultaneously utter ineffable words and perverse things. Every aggressive word swerves the Gnostic student off the royal path. Mediocre people criticize other people. Yet, the superior man criticizes himself.

Demonstrate Wisdom

Who is a wise man, endowed with knowledge among you? Let him show, out of good conversation, his works with meekness of wisdom. - James 3:13

Those who become mystically proud of their wisdom, those who boast about themselves, are like those ignoramuses who after climbing to the top of a solitary tower, start screaming and praising themselves... Therefore, those who are really wise, instead of criticizing the neighbor, let them show with good conversation, his works with meekness of wisdom.

Diabolic Wisdom

But if you have bitter envying and strife in your hearts, glory not, and lie not against the truth; this wisdom descends not from above, but is earthly, sensual and devilish. For where envying and strife is, there is confusion and every evil work.

Envy transforms any disciple into a Judas. Generally, the envious one feels to be more wise than his Master, thus he reaches the point of selling his Master for thirty coins.

> *But the wisdom that is from above is first pure, then peaceable, gentle, and easy to be intreated, full of mercy and good fruits, without partiality, and without hypocrisy. And the fruit of righteousness is sown in peace of them that make peace.* - James 3: 14-18

Word of Perfection

The perfect gentleman speaks words of perfection. Thus, any Gnostic student who wishes to tread the path must get accustomed to how to control his language. The student must be charitable with the pious handling of the word.

For example, whosoever criticizes the religion or the school or the sect of the neighbor is not charitable with the word. Indeed, he becomes cruel and merciless...

> *Hear, and understand: Not that which goes into the mouth defiles a man; but that which cometh out of the mouth, this defiles a man...!*
>
> *For out of the heart proceed evil thoughts, murders, adulteries, fornications, thefts, false witness, and blasphemies: These are the things which defile a man...*
> - Matthew 15: 10, 11, 19, 20

All religions are like precious pearls strung on the golden thread of divinity. Nonetheless, avoid all types of fanaticism because with it we cause great harm to mankind, our neighbor.

We not only hurt others with rude words or with delicate or artistic ironies but also with the tone of our voice, with an arrhythmic and disharmonious accent.

Final Word

We have reached the conclusion of this book.

Hoping that everyone who reads this book (not only the esotericist students) will resolve to enter at the narrow, strait and difficult door that leads to Light: this door is sex.

May Gnostic students remember all of the concepts of this book.

May they remember that the Akasha is sexual and that the Kundalini is precisely the same Akasha.

May they remember that the Akasha is the Goddess Kundalini, the Mother Goddess of the World.

Indeed, the blessed and adorable Mother of the world is the sacred serpent Kundalini.

This adorable serpent is enclosed within the Muladhara chakra. This chakra is located at the base of the spinal medulla. This magnetic center is sexual as shown by the evident place where it is located.

It is astounding to realize that the Muladhara chakra is located between the place where the genital organs and the anus begin.

This chakra is exactly below the Kanda and in the place where Ida, Pingala, and Sushumna join.

All of the former data indicates the sexuality of Akasha.

Whosoever wants to utter the language of the Light needs to awaken the Kundalini because the Kundalini is exactly and indubitably the concretion, or better said, the basic element of sound.

As Sivananda stated: "The Muladhara chakra is located two fingers above the anus and approximately two fingers below the genitals, thus, four fingers wide measures the space where the Muladhara chakra is located."

When the Kundalini awakens, it enters within the spinal medulla and develops throughout the length of the medullar canal. This is how the Kundalini places into activity all the seven chakras of the spinal medulla. This is how the powers over earthquakes, the waters, fire, and air are attained.

When the Kundalini reaches the larynx, then, the capacity to utter in the language of the Light is acquired.

When the Kundalini reaches the height between the eyebrows, then clairvoyance is acquired; the initiate becomes clairvoyant.

When the Kundalini ascends to the pineal gland, polyvoyance and intuition are acquired.

When the sacred, pure Akashic serpent Kundalini reaches the magnetic field of the root of the nose (where the atom of the Father is located), then the First Initiation of Major Mysteries of the great White Lodge is granted.

Notwithstanding, the entire work with the serpent belongs to *Logos, Mantra, Theurgy.*

The Word cannot be disjoined from that which is sexuality. Both Word and sex are found intimately related with absolute certainty, as it is shown by the exact place where the Muladhara chakra is located, which is the sacred abode of the pure Akasha, or the serpent called Kundalini.

In the human being, the blessed Mother Goddess of the World has the shape of a serpent.

The Soul of the world, the Anima Mundi of Plato, is enclosed within the Muladhara chakra; therefore, if we want to speak the great language of the Light, we must make the effort to raise the Kundalini throughout the central medullar canal.

Upon concluding this book, we sincerely hope that many disciples who up until now have not done anything but theorize, will find here the clue, in other words, the clue that will allow them to open the Ark of Science.

We have seen with profound pain how many brothers, thirsty for Light, search, read, scrutinize immense volumes in many libraries, yet they do not find the clue to Initiation.

We have strived to be essentially practical in this book.

This is why we have given the clue so that all those who are thirsty can quench their thirst.

We have provided the bread of wisdom, so that all those who are hungry can easily calm their hunger with this bread.

What is important is for all the brothers and sisters to study *Logos, Mantra, Theurgy* from the first to the last page with fervor, with a lot of care, and in an orderly manner.

It is indispensable that all the exercises which are written and revealed here are practiced with the utmost patience.

Lay down all gestures of impatience!

It is better to have faith, love, hope, and to practice charity!

All of us need to lift up the Son of Man within our own Selves!

May the most profound peace be with this wretched, suffering humanity!

Inverential Peace!

Toluca, Mexico, March 7, 1959

Samael Aun Weor

Esoteric Treatise of Theurgy

KING SOLOMON. ENGRAVING BY GUSTAVE DORÉ.

"When we have become cognizant
within the Internal Worlds, we can
then dedicate ourselves fully to
the works of High Theurgy."

Chapter One
Theurgy, Goeteia, and Spiritualism

Theurgy is a science that allows us to invoke the ineffable Beings of the Superior Worlds in order to receive sublime teachings from them.

Let us distinguish between Theurgy, Goeteia, and Spiritualism.

Goeteia teaches us how to invoke the purely tenebrous entities. Goeteia's invokers are enslaved by the powers of evil.

Spiritism or Spiritualism allows us to communicate with that which is beyond death. This is done through certain passive subjects (mediums). However, it is good to know that only the shadows of the deceased come into the spiritualist centers. These shadows are composed of the psychological "I" of the deceased. Therefore, it is very seldom that the Soul or the Spirit of the ones who have passed away enter into the body of a medium. Only the disincarnated psychological "I" of those who died, in other words, the shadow of our beloved relatives who died penetrates into the body of a medium... That is all.

By manifesting themselves through the mental, astral, and physical bodies of the mediums, the shadows of the deceased produce the dislocation of their mental and astral vehicles. The consequences can be insanity, paralysis, etc.

After this short preamble, we will fully enter into our superior studies of Theurgy.

The theurgist must know how to consciously travel in the Astral Body, since the theurgic invocations are performed in the Astral Plane. Invocations of High Theurgy can also be performed in the most elevated worlds of cosmic consciousness.

The theurgist must be skillful within the Astral World. The theurgist has to consciously depart within his Astral Body. Therefore, before entering the field of Theurgic invocations, we must first of all learn how to "enter" and "leave" the physical body at will.

Indeed, the Astral Body is the garment of the Soul. Within the Astral Body we have the Mind, the Will, the Conscience, and the Spirit.

There is a moment during which we can abandon our physical body at will. That moment is the state of slumber, which begins when we are falling asleep. Thus, in those moments of transition between vigil and sleep, every human being, wrapped with their Astral Body, escapes the physical body. There is a clue which allows us to consciously escape from the physical body in order to work within the Superior Worlds. The Divine Master Jesus Christ practiced this clue during his studies in the pyramid of Kefren, as follows:

When the great Master rested upon his bed (face up, horizontally), he placed the soles of his feet on the bed, thus his knees were raised. Thereafter, the Master raised his arms above his head until the palms of his hands touched, one against the other; then he extended his arms to the right and left; finally, he crossed his arms over his chest (right over left). This is how he formed the Microcosmic Star with his arms. Sequentially, the Master entered into a slumber state by vocalizing the powerful mantra "**Faraon**." This mantra is vocalized in three syllables, as follows:

Faaaaa...Raaaaa...Onnnnn...

The Master vocalized this mantra many times, until falling asleep.

This simple and easy procedure is a marvelous key, which will allow us to awaken consciousness within the Superior Worlds. Thus, this is how we awaken consciousness in the Internal Worlds. Then, we feel light... We float deliciously...

When we have become cognizant within the Internal Worlds, we can then dedicate ourselves fully to the works of High Theurgy.

Dr. Krumm-Heller advised, also, that for the exercises of Astral Body projection, it is advisable to perfume the room or bedroom with good incense, or rose essence, etc.

Chapter Two

The Conjuration of the Seven

One of the most powerful conjurations that King Solomon left us is the "Conjuration of the Seven."

We resolved to personally investigate the entire esoteric content of the "Conjuration of the Seven." We performed these investigations of High Theurgy within the Superior Worlds. We needed to have complete cognizance of the essential content of that prayer which Solomon the sage left us in ancient times.

Many magicians in the past, as well as in present, utilize these conjurations. However, in order to work consciously with them in the rituals of High Magic, we must understand the meaning of its content. This was the main motive for our in depth investigation of the esotericism of the "Conjuration of the Seven."

Sequentially, here we give to our readers the explanation of the "Conjuration of the Seven." Let us read it:

CONJURATION OF THE SEVEN OF SOLOMON THE SAGE

1. *In the name of Michael, may Jehovah command thee and drive thee hence, Chavajoth!*

2. *In the name of Gabriel, may Adonai command thee, and drive thee hence, Bael!*

3. *In the name of Raphael, begone before Elial, Samgabiel!*

4. *By Samael Sabaoth, and in the name of Elohim Gibor, get thee hence, Andrameleck!*

5. *By Zachariel et Sachiel-Meleck, be obedient unto Elvah, Sanagabril!*

6. *By the divine and human name of Shaddai, and by the sign of the Pentagram, which I hold in my right hand, in the name of the angel Anael, by the power of Adam and Eve, who are Iod-Chavah, begone Lilith! Let us rest in peace, Nahemah!*

7. *By the holy Elohim and by the names of the Genii Cashiel,*
   Sehaltiel, Aphiel and Zarahiel, at the command of Orifiel,
   depart from us Moloch! We deny thee our children to
   devour!

By carefully examining the "Conjuration of the Seven," our
beloved readers can see the style in which it is written.

Indeed, the task we had ahead of us was pretty exhaustive,
arduous, and difficult. Frankly, Spiritism (with its mediums)
would have been useless to us, since we wanted to see, touch,
and feel all the entities that are mentioned in the Conjuration
of Solomon the sage! Likewise, for us Goeteia's circle of pacts
and black evocations would have also been useless, since none
of us wanted to fall into the abyss of black magic. Therefore,
only High Theurgy could help us resolve all of these problems.

Thus, we began by studying the first conjuration in the
Superior Worlds, which literally states:

> *In the name of Michael, may Jehovah command thee*
> *and drive thee hence, Chavajoth!*

Michael is the Genie of the Sun, and any advanced occult-
ist knows this. Jehovah is the regent of the Moon; he governs
Eden, and waits for all of us in Paradise.

Therefore, we only needed to know about Chavajoth.
Who could this strange personage be? Why was it necessary to
conjure him in the name of Jehovah? Why does Michael have
to be named in this conjuration? What tenebrous entity could
Chavajoth be? Undoubtedly, all of these enigmas disquieted
us. Thus, we wanted to clarify this matter! We did not want to
continue repeating (like robots) a conjuration whose content
we ignored.

It was then that we decided to investigate.

We left our physical body at will. Thus, within our Astral
Body we all walked along a solitary road. While we walked, we
invoked Chavajoth, the mysterious personage mentioned by
the great King Solomon. We must confess that we had to utilize the grand and supreme Appellation of "Peter of Apono."

It is as follows:

HEMEN ETAN! HEMEN ETAN! HEMEN ETAN!
EL, Ati, Titeip, Azia, Hin, Teu, MINOSEL, VAY,
ACHADON, Vay, Vaa, EYE, Aaa, Eie, Exe, A EL
EL EL A Hg! HAU! HAU! HAU! HAU! Va Va Va
Va! Hg HAU HAU HAU! HAU! VA! VA! VA! VA!
CHAVAJOTH!

Aie Saraye, aie Saraye, aie Saraye! Per Eloym Archima
Raburs, Bathas Super ABRAC ruens superveniens
ABEOR SUPER ABERER, CHAVAJOTH!
CHAVAJOTH! Impero tibi per Clavem SALOMONIS
et nomen Magnus SEMHAMPHORAS.

The outcome was astounding! At the side of the road we
found a solemn, Olympic sculpture. It seemed to have been
carved by Praxiteles! Its countenance was similar to that of
the Greek Apollo. The curvature of its feet, the profile of its
hands... the entire eurhythmy of that sculpture could compete
with the Venus de Milo! Nevertheless, there was something
ominous about that very beautiful sculpture! This precious
human effigy was dressed in a blood-colored robe which had
beautiful, exotic, and fatal pleats, extending down to its feet!
We then comprehended that we were before Jehovah's opposite
pole. We were before the frightening and terrible Chavajoth!
Thus, by extending our right hand towards that malignant and
seducing beauty, we conjured it with a loud voice saying:

In the name of the Tetragrammaton, I conjure thee,
Chavajoth!

Immediately after pronouncing these words, with great
surprise we saw the beautiful and malignant sculpture become
terribly enraged with us. Then, he advanced towards us and
attacked us with his horrible, hypnotic power. Thereafter,
he exceedingly insulted us. His words were indeed revolting,
proper only for the great harlot whose number is 666.

That encounter was terrible. We had to defend ourselves
with all of our spiritual forces in order to drive away this terrible demon of malignant beauty! Thus, we finally succeeded
and the frightening personage took the form of a harlot, and

hid within a tavern where only alcoholic beverages were served at the bar.

Lo and behold black magic. Lo and behold the abyss!

After having met this personage of darkness, we returned into our physical bodies. By the color of his tunic, by his filthy language, and by all the activities of that sinister personage, we arrived at the conclusion that this was the exact antithesis of Lord Jehovah.

Now, we wanted to delve even further! We wanted to know the specific labors to which Chavajoth was dedicated.

Thus, on another night, we, the investigators, abandoned the physical body with the purpose of conversing more closely with the antithesis of Lord Jehovah. Again, we pronounced the grand Appellation of Peter of Apono. After a while, we arrived at a street in an unknown town. Multitudes of people came and went all around us. As we invoked, we could easily appreciate the power of the Word. The Word was transforming everything... We were moving from one dimension to another. We were submerging ourselves into those atomic regions, which the Princes of Darkness inhabited! By carefully observing, we noticed that someone was approaching us with a decided and firm step. It was Chavajoth! The sinister personage arrayed himself with his blood-colored robe; thus, like this he came towards us. We then conjured him as follows:

In the name of Jupiter, the Father of the Gods, I conjure thee, Chavajoth, TE VIGOS CO SLIM.

These mantras have a tremendous effect. Chavajoth, as if wounded by a mortal ray, raised his arm as if to defend himself. We advanced a few steps, came closer to him and stretched out our hand to him in a friendly gesture.

He then, in an ill-mannered tone and using expressions applicable only to prostitutes, asked us about our wives.

With serene temperaments (we did not want to be carried away by any emotional or sentimental reactions), we answered this personage and told him that our wives were quite well, thank you! Thereafter, we told him that we wanted to be his friends.

So, the sinister personage seemed satisfied. Thus, he walked with us towards his tenebrous cavern. We walked a lot until reaching the peak of a high mountain. There he has his tenebrous cavern, where he teaches his disciples. He confessed to us that he had a physical body and lived in Germany, that he worked for the grand Black Lodge and that he was impersonating a war veteran, etc.

Indeed, we found the cavern of Chavajoth crowded with German disciples. His disciples concurred in their Astral Body to the cavern. There Chavajoth taught them the doctrine of the Nicolaitanes. Such a tenebrous doctrine teaches a sinister system of Sexual Magic, during which the magician commits the crime of ejaculating the seminal liquor. The outcome of those exercises is always disastrous, because through them the fiery serpent of our magical powers, instead of rising, descends to the atomic infernos of the human being and is transformed into the tail of Satan. Chavajoth's system of black Sexual Magic was practiced by the monstrous Lemurian-Atlanteans, as well as by the sorcerers of Atlantis.

The cult to the goddess Kali existed in the vanished ancient continent of Atlantis. Later on, after its submersion, the sect of this goddess was established in India. This is the sect of the stranglers. The fanatics of that sect strangled their victims. The English police had to intervene many times in India in order to judge those types of criminals... That is Black Tantrism!

In our western world, there were many instructors who had been in the White Lodge and then went astray to the horrible path of Black Tantra.

For these reasons, we arrived at the conclusion that Chavajoth is an adept of the shadows, the antithesis of the Lord Jehovah. He is the head of a fatal legion! He works for the tenebrous fraternity. Chavajoth has to be conjured in the name of Jehovah!

Some days later, we, the investigators, in the Astral Body, decided to invoke this pair of opposites of philosophy: Jehovah and Chavajoth. We made a circle around ourselves...

The two invoked beings attended our call. The Lord Jehovah, like a dove of immaculate whiteness, hovered over our heads. Chavajoth, his antithesis, kept himself out of the circle. He was dejected! The presence of the Lord Jehovah wounded him to death...! Jehovah works for the chastity of the world. The divine wisdom of Jehovah is enclosed within the "Arcanum A.Z.F." This is the key to Eden! This is the key to the Ark of Science... Chavajoth works for Black Tantrism, for the doctrine of the Nicolaitanes, which is the fatal science that transforms humans into beasts!

Chapter Three
The Second Invocation

After having finished the esoteric investigation of the first invocation of that great "Conjuration of the Seven" (which King Solomon the Sage bequeathed to us in other times), we decided to investigate the second invocation, which literally reads as follows:

> **In the name of Gabriel, may Adonai command thee, and drive thee hence, Bael!**

We know that Gabriel is a Lunar Angel! We know that Adonai is a precious Angel!

However, we ignored who Bael could be! Why would Bael be conjured in the name of Adonai? These were enigmas for us, which we needed to resolve!

One night, while in the Astral Body, we invoked Bael. Bael was a tenebrous king who lived in a cavern in the Gobi dessert. There he instructed his disciples. He taught the black magic of the sublunar spheres. Adonai, the Son of Light and Happiness, is his opposite.

These two antitheses of philosophy are intimately related with the two rays of the Moon.

Bael's presence was awfully, exceedingly tenebrous: crowned as king, he had firm and widely spaced eyes with bushy eyebrows, a flat nose, thick lips, and a round face. He was dressed in the robe of a black magician. Wounded by our conjuration, he trembled before us. We could not establish a friendship with him because his character was unapproachable.

On another night, we, the investigators, invoked Adonai, Son of Light and Happiness. He who resembled an infant of a few months old attended our call; he attacked us with a sinister and terrible force! We had to appeal to all of our psychic and spiritual forces to try to overcome him. However, everything was useless! That child was endowed with an omnipotent force...! Then, someone told us to stretch out our hand to him in a friendly manner and so we did. We stretched out our hand towards him with the intention of greeting him. He then fraternally answered our greeting and shook our hand. This was the Guardian of the Threshold of the Angel Adonai, Son of Light and Happiness.

What is most intriguing is to think that the Angel Adonai (who in spite of his immense perfection) still conserves the Guardian of the Threshold, the psychological "I," the reincarnating ego that we must all decapitate and dissolve in order to incarnate the Internal Christ within us.

How difficult it is to achieve perfection.

An Angel as precious as Adonai, and yet, it is hard to even think that he still continues with the psychological "I" (a bunch of old memories...).

On another night, the most profound night, the quietest night... we, the investigators, invoked the Angel Adonai. The precious Angel sent us a divine gift (with other Angels). It was a medallion, which hung from a golden chain! Such a medallion confers upon us the power to switch cosmic planes instantaneously. With that precious treasure we can enter into any department of the Kingdom. We established a very good friendship with the precious Angel Adonai, the Son of Light and Happiness, the Master of Zanoni.

We all know that Zanoni received his cosmic Initiation in the Tower of Fire in the ancient Chaldea of the sages. Since then, Zanoni received the Elixir of Long Life and was able to preserve his same physical body for millions of years... Nonetheless, the great Master Zanoni allowed himself to fall; he fell in love with an artist from Naples! Thus, the outcome of his error was the guillotine, which is where the great Master died!

We the investigators, learned many things, ineffable wisdom from the Angel Adonai.

On a certain occasion, Adonai, the Son of Light and Happiness, and the Master Zanoni, came to us. Waiting, one of us became somewhat astonished when both Adonai and

Zanoni told the astonished investigator to cut a strange thread that was on the ground with his sword. Thus, the astonished investigator, between perplexity and happiness, obeyed and cut the thread with his flaming sword. Once this work was accomplished, we understood that he had been liberated from some fatal sorcery, from a bad current, from an act of black magic... Someone had harmed him with those evil arts, and had caused him great harm.

Thereafter, both the Master Zanoni and Adonai healed the investigator's Astral Body and cured him.

As for king Bael, through subsequent works we had to submerge him into the Abyss (we were obeying supreme orders). That tenebrous personage used his powers in order to cause great harm to humanity. Indeed, Bael is the head of a legion, and must be conjured in the name of his antithesis, Adonai, the Son of Light and Happiness.

To end this chapter, we must warn the imprudent to never invoke the tenebrous ones because this is extremely dangerous...! We needed to invoke those tenebrous entities in order to investigate the "Conjuration of the Seven" of King Solomon the sage; this was an important matter, this is why we had to perform these types of investigations. These types of tenebrous entities are invoked with the Conjuration of Peter of Apono.

Nevertheless, we warn you that the Angels of Light, the Ineffable Beings, cannot be invoked with the Appellation of Peter of Apono. Angels must be invoked in the name of Christ, by the power of Christ, by the glory of Christ.

May the imprudent be careful! May they not commit the error of invoking demons, because this could lead them to disgrace! If we the investigators were able to perform these investigations it is because we are very skillful in the use and maneuvering of the Astral Body.

Nevertheless, we always found ourselves in great and terrible danger!

Raphael Teaches Tobias about Sexual Magic [Read the apocryphal book of Tobit]

Chapter Four
The Third Invocation

After having investigated the former invocations, we decided to study the third invocation of the "Conjuration of the Seven," which states the following:

In the name of Raphael, begone before Elial, Samgabiel!

When we investigated Samgabiel (do not confuse this name with Saint Gabriel) we met a terrible demon of the world of the Cosmic Mind. The Angel Elial is his exact divine and ineffable opposite.

Later, on another day, we invoked Raphael... Then the grand Master attended our call. The Master carried the trident of the Mental World in his right hand. His face was rosy like fire. His white beard rested on his chest; it was filled with majesty and light. The wide forehead of the Master portrayed for us his profound wisdom. One amongst us asked the grand Master for something. The Master answered the following:

"You no longer need to ask for anything!"

Indeed, that supplicant was an Initiate with complete knowledge of the Science of Good and Evil.

We must distinguish between the Master and his Human Soul. The Master is the inner God.

It will be of great astonishment for our readers to know that the human soul of this grand Master (the Bodhisattva Raphael) has a physical body. What is the most grave in this matter is to know that the Human Soul of this Master is now fallen... his Bodhisattva... is fallen! However, he is struggling terribly in order to rise...

Many extremely dangerous demons live in the world of the Cosmic Mind! On a certain occasion, we entered a very luminous temple of the world of the mind. All of us, the investigators, were functioning with our Mental Body. In that temple, there was a venerable group of elders. They were dressed in the robes of Masters. They wore sandals. Their white hair fell over their shoulders in beautiful curls. Their long white beards and their wide foreheads gave those elders a magnificent appearance. We, the investigators, believed that we were in a temple of White Magic, before a group of Holy Masters. That was the belief we had! One of those elders pronounced an ineffable speech.

He spoke of sublime things. He spoke divinely. He spoke of love, goodness, beauty, charity, etc. Suddenly, the grand Master began to delicately touch the problem of sex. Then, in a sublime way he said:

"Be fruitful, and multiply; the sexual act is nothing bad, seminal ejaculation is not bad, it is necessary for reproduction, because God said: "Be fruitful, and multiply!" (Genesis 1:28)

This and many other terms were used by that venerable elder, to defend seminal ejaculation. It was then that we began to suspect the sanctity of that "saint." We began to doubt... could this elder be a black magician? However, when looking around us, we only saw venerable elders... splendorous light! Ineffable things... It even seemed a sacrilege to us to doubt this Master and such a holy place! However, the mortifying doubt, in spite of everything, in spite of all our reasoning, continued to afflict us deeply. Then, at this moment one of us, wanting to clear up these doubts, stood up and exclaimed the following phrases: "Hail to the Christ! Down with Javhe!

Christ and Javhe are the two antitheses. Light and Darkness! White Magic and Black Magic...! Javhe is that demon that tempted Christ on the mountain. Javhe is a terribly perverse demon! He is the Chief of the black magistracy.

So, when we shouted, "Hail to Christ," and "Down with Javhe," that Black Lodge, filled with anger, and became enraged with us. Black magicians adore Javhe; they follow Javhe... Thus, this is what happened that night within that temple in the world of the mind!

When those apparently "holy" men (with venerable and august appearances) heard that "Hail to Christ," and "Down with Javhe," something horrible happened... suddenly, the apparently "holy" face of that venerable elder that spoke to us was completely disturbed, it became totally enraged and distorted...

It was then when we beheld the unsuspected, the unmasked elder with his horrible countenance joined the rest of "holy" elders who completely unmasked themselves; they were true princes of darkness, terrible black magicians of the world of the Cosmic Mind! They insulted us with phrases and words proper only to the great harlot whose number is 666. Thus, they attacked us violently...

We had to unsheathe the flaming sword in order to defend ourselves! Later, we left that den of black magic, which in the beginning we thought was a temple of sanctity...

"In the name of Jupiter, the
father of the Gods, I conjure thee
Andrameleck! TE VIGOS CO SLIM!"

Chapter Five

The Fourth Invocation

Continuing with our investigations of High Theurgy, we will now study the fourth invocation of the "Conjuration of the Seven." This invocation is as follows:

> *By Samael Sabaoth, and in the name of Elohim Gibor, get thee hence, Andrameleck!*

Who could Andrameleck be? Who could Elohim Gibor be? Why are these genii mentioned in this fourth conjuration of King Solomon? All these enigmas disquieted us. Only by means of High Theurgy can these types of investigation be done.

Samael is the Genie of Mars. But who could Elohim Gibor and Andrameleck be?

One night, we projected ourselves in the Astral Body; thus, we entered a subterranean cavern. Once there, by making use of the grand Appellation of Peter of Apono, we invoked Andrameleck. For a long time we remained performing the invocation within that subterranean cavern of the Earth.

Finally, a personage, black as coal, appeared in the middle of that cavern; it was a gigantic personage, tenebrous and horrible. By extending our right hand towards that horrible monster, we exclaimed:

> *In the name of Jupiter, the father of the Gods, I conjure thee Andrameleck! TE VIGOS CO SLIM!*

The outcome was astounding. That demon, mortally wounded by the terrible ray of divine justice, remained under our dominion. It was then that Andrameleck spoke and said, "I did not know that you were the one calling me! If I had known it, I would have come earlier! What is it that I can do for you?"

These words uttered by Andrameleck seemed to blare from within the profound caverns of the entire Earth. It seemed that his terrible and powerful voice blared from within the very inner center of the Earth! We then courageously spoke to Andrameleck as follows, "Give me your hand, Andrameleck!"

The tenebrous personage drew near onto us in order to greet us with his hand. Then the author of this book returned into his physical body. Then, that demon, with his blood-red-colored robe, passed over the roof of my house and exclaimed, "You were afraid of me! You were afraid of me!"

I answered, "I am not afraid of you, Andrameleck! I just returned into my body, that is all."

Another night, a group of brothers, in our Astral Bodies met in a temple in order to continue our investigation in relation with that mysterious personage, Andrameleck, mentioned by Solomon the sage in the "Conjuration of the Seven."

By applying Peter of Apono's formula, we, the brothers, all made a great chain in order to invoke Andrameleck. After a period of invocations, we heard Andrameleck's answer in the distance. A strange, profoundly frozen wind! A hurricane blew near to us! That personage modulated the vowel "M." He gave a special intonation with low and high tones to that letter... The brothers remained firm in the chain. Suddenly, one of the brothers who directed the chain exclaimed with a loud voice: "Brethren, do not release the chain! Remain firm! Andrameleck is approaching!"

Some moments later, a giant appeared at the threshold (entrance) of the door. That giant was about three or four meters tall. That strange personage wore a black robe, yet, a white strip fell obliquely from his right shoulder down to his left thigh, passing on the front and on the back. He had a huge medallion on his chest and was carrying a scepter of command in his right hand. That personage had a wide forehead, big blue eyes, which were reflecting the starry heaven; his nose was straight, he had fine, delicate lips, white hands, with cone shaped fingers. His elongated hands had the mystical contour similar to those hands of Jesus of Nazareth or Francis of Assisi... The brother who was leading the chain released it and drew near to Andrameleck in order to embrace and greet him.

Thereafter, he turned towards the brethren of the chain and told them, "Brethren, allow me to introduce my friend Andrameleck to you!"

All the brethren were trembling. One of them, being incapable of resisting the terrible electric force radiated by the eyes of Andrameleck, hastily left. Terrified, he ran away!

Such a marvelous giant, filled with a great decency and with courteous and delicate manners, stretched out his hand in order to courteously greet each and every one of the brethren. Afterwards, he drew near to a desk, and sat on a chair before the desk. It was quite remarkable to contemplate that strange giant, possessing so much courtesy, so much decency, and so much harmony. Yet, it caused melancholy to see the profoundness behind that marvelous giant, in other words, the seeming memory of a fatal shadow. Nonetheless, the scepter, which that giant carried, the medallion on his chest, and all his gestures, were really of the White Lodge. Thus, seated before the desk, Andrameleck called the brother who led the chain and advised him with the following words:

"Exert yourself, brother... Place yourself in the best possible environment. Dress decently! You must comprehend that we are Angels and therefore, we have the full right to live well!"

Then the interlocutor brother asked Andrameleck for his consent as follows:

"Master, excuse me, I have to go and look for brother X" (the brother who left the temple earlier)

Thus, the brother who directed the chain left, in the Astral Body, traveling to all the countries of the Earth, looking for the brother who had fled. He wanted that brother to speak to Andrameleck. Yet, it was useless! Such a search was fruitless... Brother X was nowhere to be found! Where could he be? Where could he have gone? Enigmas, enigmas!

Thus, the brother who was the director of the chain returned once again to the temple where Andrameleck was. However, it was no longer possible for him to talk to that marvelous giant, because many people (in their Astral Bodies) were consulting him. Then, the brother who directed the chain returned to his physical body.

Once within his body, that brother rose very early in the morning, ate his breakfast and left for the street... in search of brother X.

Well then, beloved reader, allow me to tell you now that the director of the chain went in search of brother X, who in the physical plane was an old businessman; thus, it was very easy for the director of the chain to find him in his store. Certainly, he found him there!

Brother X was busy attending to the commerce of his store. The director of the chain, after courteously greeting his friend, questioned him as follows, "Well, brother, tell me why you fled from Andrameleck's sight?"

Then brother X answered him, "Indeed, I could not resist Andrameleck's sight! He looked at me with a terrible electric force! I could not bear it! I was afraid and I fled!"

It was then that the director of the chain asked brother X, "Man, I looked for you in the Astral Body everywhere, and I did not find you!"

Brother X responded, "You did not find me because I returned to my body!"

That whole Sunday, the two men discussed the matter of Andrameleck. That giant was an enigma to the two investigators. Could Andrameleck be a black magician? Could Andrameleck be a white magician? Enigmas! Enigmas! Enigmas!

Indeed, that entire matter was enigmatic. The two men decided, each on his own, to investigate Andrameleck.

Thus, after some time, they came to the following conclusion:

The Spirit who attended the chain was really the Master Andrameleck. A Master of the White Lodge! A Master of Major Mysteries! It so happened that this Master sent his Bodhisattva (his Human Soul) to reincarnate!

Remember that the Spirit *is* and the Soul is *acquired*. Thus, the Soul, the Bodhisattva, reincarnated in China. Unfortunately, this Bodhisattva allowed himself to fall!

Lo and behold, the mystery of the "double human personality," one of the major mysteries of occultism. Bodhisattvas fall because of **sex**! They fornicate. They ejaculate the seminal liquor. Thus, this is how the fiery serpent of our magical powers, the Kundalini, descends towards the atomic infernos of the Human Being. This is how Bodhisattvas fall... Nonetheless, the Master, in other words, the Innermost, the Spirit can never fall. Therefore, the one who fell was the Bodhisattva of the Master Andrameleck!

What is worse regarding this Bodhisattva is that he dedicated himself to black magic. The outcome of all this conduct was that the Master withdrew his Will-Soul, Human Soul, the Fifth Principle of the Human Being, the Causal Body or Superior Manas of Theosophy.

Thereafter, only the inferior quaternary formed by the Physical, Ethereal, Astral, and Mental vehicles was left living in China. Such an inferior quaternary is, in fact, a soulless entity, a Kabbalistic cortex... an empty shell where the Soul no longer lives, where the immortal principle of every human being no longer inhabits! These Kabbalistic cortexes are abodes of the psychological I (Satan). Indeed... these are demons!

Therefore, that man transformed himself into a demon! Thus, when the Investigator invokes Andrameleck in the Astral, Andrameleck, the demon, or Andrameleck, the grand spiritual Master, can appear.

Much later, we, the investigators invoked Andrameleck and Elohim Gibor. They appeared to our call. We then saw the two antitheses face to face! Elohim Gibor is the antithesis of the tenebrous Andrameleck. Elohim Gibor is a full Archangel of the Ray of Mars! He carries the flaming sword at his waist, and is a terribly divine male.

When Andrameleck attacked us, we overcame him easily. Then, lying in his bed of pain, he told us that in China, he used a small ampoule named KINOCAPOL, with which he instantly awakens the clairvoyance in his disciples (of course, this type of clairvoyance only lasts as long as the effect of the injection! That is all). The demon Andrameleck is a businessman in

China! He lives economically well. This personage of darkness lives in the Abyss.

After hearing this story, a friend of ours asked us the following, "Therefore, Andrameleck no longer has an Innermost? When he passes away, will he only ascend to the Causal Plane? Will he have another body in another reincarnation?"

We then answered the following, "Andrameleck no longer has a physical body. The giant who came to the chain was precisely the Innermost of Andrameleck. That Innermost no longer has any relationship with the tenebrous man who lives in China. When the man Andrameleck (who lives in China) passes away, then this soulless monster will not be able to rise to the Causal Plane, nor to the Superior Worlds, because he is a "Soulless" entity; he is a Kabbalistic shell, an empty house. He does not have a Soul, nor does he have a Spirit.

"Those Kabbalistic cortexes sink into the atomic infernos of Nature for centuries; little by little they degenerate and lose strength. Later they take the form of horrible animals of the Abyss, afterwards, the form of plants and finally, mineral form, which in the process of disintegration will be deprived of intelligence. Thus, finally, they become cosmic dust! This is the "Second Death" mentioned in the Apocalypse (Book of Revelation).

"Fornicators, in the end, after all, have to pass through the "Second Death." Fornicators are people of black magic! Whosoever ejaculates the seminal liquor is a fornicator, and a sure candidate for the Abyss and the "Second Death."

"Andrameleck will become cosmic dust within the Abyss. Disintegration in the Abyss is very slow and dreadful. Many times, those tenebrous ones sustain themselves for eternities, during entire Cosmic Days and Nights. Yet, they disintegrate little by little and finally die!

"Andrameleck will not have a physical body again! He is a terribly perverse demon. The Internal Master suffered horribly, and of course, he will have to pay a great Karma for having created that demon."

Our interlocutor then asked us the following question,
"Is the Innermost Andrameleck guilty of the evil deeds of
Andrameleck the demon and of the karma which this demon
has to pay?"

We had to answer him as follows, "The Innermost is an
Immolated Lamb and will have to pay for that Tantric ex-personality! The Innermost, the Inner Master, will have to reincarnate in order to pay the karma of his ex-personality. The Law
is the Law. That Master lacked the strength in order to control
that tenebrous human personality. When the Spirit overcomes
matter, he is victorious. That is all..."

"The Angels are filled with light and fire
because they are absolutely chaste."

Chapter Six

The Fifth Invocation

The readers who have closely followed the entire course of our investigations will comprehend that Spiritism or Spiritualism with its mediums or necromancy with its laboratories would not have helped us in performing these transcendental invocations of High Theurgy.

There are many students who would like to see, hear, touch and feel these things, but regrettably, their complementary faculties are damaged.

There are many people who would like to consciously project themselves in their Astral Body; yet, they suffer the unspeakable because they do not achieve it.

The clue, which we gave in our first chapter, namely the mantra "**Faraon**," is formidable; it is important to never give up, to persevere, to not become tired of practicing it until you reach success.

During the normal hours of sleep, every human being is outside of the physical body. In the Internal Worlds, our Innermost intervenes in order to make us integrally comprehend all of the processes of our daily life; for instance, business that we performed during the day, words that we uttered, emotions we experienced, etc.

It is unfortunate that we live unconsciously daily. We do not comprehend the threefold range (physically, soulfully, and spiritually) of each of our daily actions, of each of our words, of each sentiment. This is why our Innermost intervenes during our sleep in order to make us see symbolically the threefold range of all the events that we perform during our daily life. Thus, during sleep, human souls move within those symbols. These symbols are the so-called dreams.

If we lived completely conscious of each of the actions of our daily life, if we comprehended the threefold range of each action of our daily life, if before going to sleep we performed a retrospective exercise in order to become totally and absolutely "cognizant of our consciousness" in regards to all of the events that occurred during the day, then during the hours of normal sleep we would be absolutely free, as if we were on a "vacation." We would move completely conscious in our Astral Body; we would act with an awakened consciousness within the Internal Worlds.

Notwithstanding, we must warn that the retrospective exercise must be performed during profound meditation. We must recognize our errors, to repent for them, to have the resolution to not repeat those errors, to not condemn our errors, nor justify them. When we condemn or justify an error, we do not comprehend it; what is important is to consciously comprehend them. When we become totally and absolutely "cognizant of our consciousness" trapped within a certain defect, then that defect disintegrates. We remain free of it! Therefore, the important thing is for the dreamer to awaken within the Internal Worlds during normal sleep, during the nocturnal sleep, without "mediumistic trances," without "hypnotism," etc.

After this preamble to our present chapter, let us now continue with the investigations of the "Conjuration of the Seven." After having taken care of the previous investigations, we decided to study the "fifth conjuration" of the great King Solomon within the Superior Worlds.

Let us read:

> **By Zachariel et Sachiel-Meleck, be obedient unto Elvah, Sanagabril!**

We already knew that Zachariel is the Genie of Jupiter. What we didn't know was who Elvah and Sanagabril were. At first glance, we comprehended that they were the two antitheses of the Ray of Jupiter. Sanagabril had to be called with the Appellation of Peter of Apono because he was a tenebrous entity. Since Sanagabril has to be conjured in order to drive him away, it is logical that he is a tenebrous one. As for Elvah, we inferred that he was a luminous Angel, since he has to be named in order to drive away Sanagabril. Therefore, Elvah

could not be invoked with the Appellation of Peter of Apono.
We can only call him in the name of Christ, by the majesty of
Christ, by the power of Christ.

Thus, in the Internal Worlds, we began to invoke
Sanagabril. Within a small hall (while in the Astral Body) we
made the invocation. We called many times, yet Sanagabril was
delayed. A narrow corridor, a long passageway full of darkness
led to the small room where we were performing the invocation. After a period of patient waiting, we felt the steps of
someone coming through the narrow corridor. Indeed, those
footsteps were not very pleasant! The sounds of those steps
were not of shoes or sandals. It was a different sound. It was
the sound of claws and nails, like that of a tiger, or of an evil
beast.

We remained firm. We waited for Sanagabril to draw a
little closer. We were prepared to conjure him with a mighty
force! Suddenly, a strange being came to the threshold of that
dwelling. Then, we looked and saw such a horrible face, which
only the imagination of somebody who is mad as a hatter
or a half-wit would be able to conceive. It would have been
better for us if we saw the dead coming out of their tombs at
midnight, than to contemplate the tremendously horrible face
of Sanagabril! Frankly, the terrible aspect of such a diabolical beast surprised us so much, that the impression caused
us to instantaneously return back to our physical bodies. We
were not afraid of him! His horrible ugliness astounded us...
Everyone who follows the black path arrives at that dismal
state!

Nevertheless, we were not dismayed. Thus, we decided to
confront the horrendous spectacle again.

Therefore, on another night while in our Astral Body,
with certainty of spirit, we once again did the invocation of
Sanagabril. This time we invoked him on a street corner in a
large city. Sanagabril came to our call! He was anxious to talk
to us and took the shape of a normal man; he looked like a
banker, and arrived talking to us about money. He gave us the
prize-winning numbers of the lottery, so that we might buy a

ticket... With these temptations, he tried to attract us to his sphere of tenebrous influence. Lottery is pure black magic! An entire population is robbed in order to enrich a few. We did not allow ourselves to become imprisoned within that "little golden cage." We were only interested in knowing this tenebrous aspect, this shadow of Jupiter!

Thereafter, on another night, we decided to investigate Elvah. This Angel is love, altruism, charity, chastity, and sanctity!

Chapter Seven
The Sixth Invocation

The path of High Theurgy allows us to study the great mysteries of life and death.

However, it is necessary to learn how to consciously travel in the Astral Body. Therefore, those who still do not have that faculty and want to attain it need to acquire it through daily and vigorous training.

At the precise moment of awakening from normal sleep, after returning into the physical body and awakening in bed, many students commit the error of moving their bodies. They ignore that with this movement, the Astral Body becomes agitated and memories are lost. Therefore, when awakening from normal sleep, the student of occultism must not move! We must remain resting, with our eyes closed, and perform a retrospective exercise in order to remember (in detail) all the places we were while in the Astral Body, all the words that we heard, that we said, etc.

Understand that for these types of investigations, the mediums of Spiritism or Spiritualism are useless. It so happens that mediums do not have enough mental equilibrium. Mediums are victims of tenebrous entities. Mediums have their Mental Body dislocated; actually, the Mental and Astral Bodies of mediums are dislocated. Thus, because mediums have these two vehicles in such a condition, they cannot possess the necessary mental equilibrium and the exact logic in order to investigate the causes and effects of Nature.

We already know that the laws of Nature are wisely processed. Every effect has its cause. Every cause is the effect of another superior cause.

We have frequently heard of so many unbalanced individuals who state that they "channel" entities from beyond! Usually, those "channelers" are mediums.

Notwithstanding, it is necessary to know that the investigator of the Superior Worlds must possess a faultless mental equilibrium for this purpose. The true investigator is profoundly analytical and rigorously exact. We are mathematical in investigation and very demanding in expression.

After this preamble to our present chapter, we will narrate to our readers the investigation we performed regarding the "sixth invocation" of the great King Solomon.

This invocation is as follows:

> **By the divine and human name of Shaddai and by the sign of the Pentagram which I hold in my right hand, in the name of the Angel Anael, by the power of Adam and Eve, who are Iod-Chavah, begone Lilith! Let us rest in peace, Nahemah!**

Who could Lilith be? Who could Nahemah be? Why was it necessary to conjure these tenebrous ones in the name of the Angel Anael, the Angel of Love, and by the powers of Adam and Eve who are Iod-Chavah?

We wanted to know the Angel Anael, the Angel of Love. Therefore, we, a group of brethren in the Astral Body, invoked the Angel Anael in the name of Christ, by the majesty of Christ, by the power of Christ. Holding hands we formed a chain, and thus we made the invocation inside the patio of a house. It was at the hour of the morning aurora. Thus, with a great voice, we invoked the Angel of Love. After some time, very high above we saw a few ineffable birds passing over the patio of the house; these were silver birds! Golden birds! Birds of fire! One amongst them, the most beautiful, was Anael, the Angel of Love, who in his Astral Body had assumed that beautiful figure. All of us exclaimed, "Here he comes; here is Anael, the Angel of Love!"

We waited for those marvelous and divine birds to descend to the patio of the house where all of us brethren had made the invocation of High Theurgy. However, in rapid flight those birds passed by and did not descend to the patio of the house. Why? What could have happened?

Suddenly, someone rhythmically knocked three times at the door of the house. Thus, in our astral bodies, we released the chain and went to open the door. A beautiful boy, dressed in a pink and blue tunic, presented himself at the threshold. Other children followed him. This beautiful boy was Anael, the Angel of Love, the Angel of the Dawn, the Angel of Venus! The hair of that child looked like a golden cascade falling over his ineffable back. He looked like a twelve-year-old boy. His face, as rosy as the aurora, had ineffable and perfect facial features. His whole body was as rosy as the aurora. The boy carried flowers in his arms. We knelt down so that he would bless us, and he did! In the presence of such a beautiful boy, one only feels like playing; one feels revived to infancy; one feels like becoming a child again!

On his knees before the Angel of Love, the director of the chain consulted him about something. The boy answered him with great wisdom. We carefully observed the aura of that Angel: it is white, pure, innocent and perfect. The Angel Anael radiates splendorous light, divine light, and ineffable light! Such a precious light radiates from his spinal medulla...

Indeed, the spinal medulla is the candelabra with seven arms of the temple. The pure golden oil of the candelabra is the Christonic semen (which fornicators miserably ejaculate). The demons are filled with darkness because they spill the semen miserably.

Yet, the Angels are filled with light and fire because they are absolutely chaste.

In order to create, it is not necessary to ejaculate the seminal liquor. The seed always passes through into the uterus without the need of ejaculating the semen. The multiple combinations of this infinite substance (the semen) are marvelous.

So, after we invoked the Angel Anael, we decided to meet Lilith, his tenebrous antithesis.

Thus, on another night, a most calm one... a most silent one... we simultaneously invoked Anael and Lilith. We made the invocation while in the Astral Body, within a small room. After a few moments, the Angel Anael came to our call. The beautiful boy had an ineffable appearance. We knelt, and he blessed us. Thereafter, the boy sat on a chair and we, filled with immense veneration, and with profound respect, asked the boy the favor of invoking Lilith, his antithesis.

We asked him, "Master, invoke Lilith for us; we are investigating the pairs of opposites of philosophy." Then, the Angel Anael mentally invoked his antithesis... Outside, we heard some steps. In a few moments, another boy (the exact size of Anael, the Angel of Love) entered the room. He was Lilith; he was the antithesis of Anael!

Thus, that night we saw a terribly malignant boy, a boy with a terribly perverse face! That boy wore a black and dark blue tunic. Those are the colors of the infrared range. These same colors are used by the White Lodge but within the ultraviolet range.

Infrared colors are of the Black Lodge! Ultraviolet color is of the White Lodge.

Lilith is a demon, and his clothes are those of a demon. Lilith is a terrible fornicator! His spinal medulla only radiates abysses and darkness.

We, the investigators, offered a chair to Lilith so that he would sit. The chair was placed in front of the Angel Anael. Thus, this is how the two antitheses of Venus sat face to face. It was something admirable to see these two antitheses face to face... Anael and Lilith! In ancient times, Iamblichus, the theurgist, caused Love and Anti-love to appear before the crowds. There they were, Love and Anti-love, face to face!

Lilith did not dare to look at the severe, radiant, and luminous face of Anael. We then exclaimed, "Lo and behold, this is the mystery of the twin souls! Lo and behold, the pair of opposites of philosophy!" (Editor's Note: there are various types of twin souls).

We were inebriated with wisdom; we were experiencing an authentic state of remarkable mystical exaltation!

Lilith and Nahemah are two terribly perverse demons. These two demons govern the spheres of the Abyss.

In his third message of the Aryavarta Ashram about the Sacred Order of Tibet, the Master Hilarion IX textually states the following:

> "Kabbalists state that within the infernos there are two Kingdoms of the Strigias, namely: Lilith, the mother of abortions, and Nahemah, fatal and mortal beauty. When a man is unfaithful to his wife, which heaven had given him, and delivers himself to the licentiousness of sterile passion, then God takes away his rightful wife and throws him into the arms of Nahemah. This queen of the Strigias knows how to seduce him with all the enchantments of virginity and love. She leads the hearts of fathers astray, pushing them to abandon their children; she makes married people dream about becoming widows, and has those who are consecrated to God dream about marriage. When she usurps the title of wife, it is easy to recognize her, since she appears bald on her wedding day, since the long hair (the veil of decency in women) is intercepted on that day. After the wedding, she becomes the prisoner of despair and becomes weary of existing. Thus, she preaches suicide and finally, she violently abandons the home, leaving her victim marked with an infernal star between his eyes. Tradition adds that when sex controls the brain, this star is inverted (the Pentagonal Star) and the victim falls upside down, with his legs raised and agitating in the air. Thus, this is why the picture of the "Fool" appears on one of the 78 cards of the Bohemian Tarot. Notwithstanding, when profane science has frequently considered the Initiates to be madmen, we are satisfied knowing the evident fact that profane science is incapable of distinguishing between a fall and a descent. The alienist completely ignores the real existence of Adam Protoplastos."

In the Abyss, Lilith and Nahemah live in an eternal struggle. The depraved souls of Lilith no longer have any possibility of redemption, whilst the victims of Nahemah still have the possibility of leaving the abyss. The problem to resolve is sexual. Demons are terrible fornicators!

The five-pointed star symbolizes the human being. The brain must control sex. When the brain can no longer control sex, then the pentagonal star becomes inverted, and the human being sinks into the Abyss. Demons can be symbolized with the inverted pentagonal star.

Chapter Eight

The Seventh Invocation

After having investigated the six preceding invocations of the great "Conjuration of the Seven," which the great King Solomon left to us in ancient times, we decided to investigate the last invocation, which literally states:

> **By the Holy Elohim and by the names of the genii Cashiel, Sehaltiel, Aphiel, and Zarahiel, at the command of Orifiel, depart from us Moloch! We deny thee our children to devour.**

Who could this Moloch be? Ancient tradition tells us about Moloch, an iron bull that was heated red-hot. The story tells us that many children were thrown into the horrible stomach of this iron bull. So, much has been stated about Moloch, and we wanted to investigate this case.

Thus, outside the physical body, we invoked Moloch with the grand Appellation of Peter of Apono. So as we vocalized the mantras, we sunk into the atomic infernos of Nature and there we saw the immense multitudes of human beings who live in those Abysses.

Suddenly, we saw a rider on a horse, riding in the midst of those multitudes; the rider came mounted on a vigorous stallion.

That rider looked like someone from Arabia. He wore a blood-colored robe and covered his head with an oriental turban. Indeed, the face of that man looked like that of an Arab: his penetrating eyes were large and black with bushy eyebrows, strong and thick lips, a straight nose, dark colored.

The man wore sandals. Indeed, his entire appearance was like that of a rider from pleasant Arabia. He was Moloch! The terrible demon Moloch! Hastily, opening his way among the multitudes, he came towards us riding his vigorous stallion. He addressed the director of the chain of investigations, by mockingly shouting in a loud voice. Perversely satisfied, he told him the following, "Ah...! I thought you were up there, among the little Angels! So, you came back, eh?!"

Then the director of the great chain of investigations, courageously answered him, "You are mistaken, Moloch. I am not here to stay, only to visit. I have come down only to investigate you. That is all!"

Moloch withdrew. Thereafter, all of us investigators returned into our physical bodies. Much later, we invoked Orifiel, the angel of Saturn, who is the luminous antithesis of this demon.

That angel Orifiel governs the marvelous Ray of Saturn.

After we concluded the investigation of this last invocation of the "Conjuration of the Seven," we arrived at the following conclusions:

1st: The "Conjuration of the Seven" of Solomon the sage is a Kabbalistic conjuration of immense power in order to combat the tenebrous legions.

2nd: The "Conjuration of the Seven" of Solomon the sage should be utilized by all students of occultism before their rituals, or in order to "cleanse" their homes, or before going to sleep, or before doing their esoteric exercises. Thus, this is how the tenebrous ones are driven away.

3rd: Demons are terrible fornicators since they ejaculate the seminal liquor.

4th: Angels never ever ejaculate the seminal liquor.

5th: When human beings do not ejaculate their seminal liquor, they awaken the Kundalini, the fiery serpent of our magical powers which is enclosed in the coccygeal chakra (the church of Ephesus), at the base of the spinal medulla, which in common and ordinary people is closed. The seminal vapors open this orifice so that the fiery serpent may enter through there. As the serpent rises through the medullar channel, it opens up all of our powers, developing all of our faculties. The first great Initiation of Fire is attained when the serpent reaches the area between our eyebrows after having passed over the top of our head. We have to work with the seven degrees of the power of fire; this is how the human being is transformed into an authentic Angel, filled with power and glory!

6th: When human beings ejaculate their seminal liquor through the practices of black magic, when they follow the doctrine of the Nicolaitanes, or simply, when they never repent of ejaculating the seminal liquor, then the fiery serpent of our magical powers descends into the atomic infernos of the human being (instead of rising through the medullar canal) and becomes the horrible tail of Satan (the Kundabuffer).

7th: It is dreadfully dangerous to invoke demons. We found ourselves in very serious and tremendous danger when we were performing the investigation of the "Conjuration of the Seven!" If the student is not armed with the Sword of Justice, if he is not absolutely chaste, if he does not follow the path of sanctification, he could easily lose his life in those works, or just as well, could arrive at the most terrible despair, the most frightening fear, with very serious consequences for the physical body, risking himself by invoking demons.

8th: High Theurgy must only be utilized in order to invoke Angels. By means of High Theurgy, we can study at the feet of the Grand Master of Wisdom, converse with the Angels, talk with the constructors of the universe, talk with our inner God, face to face, in the Superior Worlds.

9th: We must sublimate all of our sexual energies towards the heart. We must tread the path of absolute sanctity.

10th: After having visited the Abyss, we arrived at the conclusion that the demons disintegrate in the Abyss within the most frightening and horrible suffering. This is the "Second Death!"

"The Third Logos radiates his energy
in the fundamental vortex of every
nebula, in the center of the smallest
atom, in everything that comes to life."

Final Conclusion

We, the investigators, while in the Astral Body, arrived at a house where one could only see mud, misery, indigence, hunger, and worst of all... terrible fornication!

We saw a horrible, repugnant room; a terribly fornicating woman lived in that room. That woman had already died; she had already entered the Abyss! In that filthy room in which she lived, only rags, mud, indigence, misery, suffering, and dirt could be seen. When we were investigating, we were able to intuitively see the close relationship that exists between the tenebrous powers featured in the "Conjuration of the Seven" and fornicating people.

The whole of this is one and the same thing: Black magic! Fornication! Repugnant misery! We, the investigators, were able to see that incorrigible fornicators pay their karma through the most atrocious misery, the most disconcerting and horrible misery in their last reincarnations.

Whosoever ejaculates their seminal liquor, even if they are married, are violators of the Law; they are fornicators!

The soul of any fornicator (before entering into the Abyss) receives the last physical body and lives in the most frightening and terrible misery. So, fornicators sink into those tenebrous regions after their last reincarnation filled with the most repugnant indigence ever known by human generation. In the Orient, the Abyss, or the atomic infernos of Nature are known with the term of Avitchi. All sins will be forgiven EXCEPT the sin against the Holy Spirit! The sexual energy is the creative energy of the Third Logos. The Third Logos is the Holy Spirit. The Third Logos radiates his energy in the fundamental vortex of every nebula, in the center of the smallest atom, in everything that comes to life. In the human being, the energy of the Third Logos is the creative power of sex.

When human beings dedicate themselves to fornication, their creative energy becomes outwardly and downwardly exteriorized, thus connecting them to the tenebrous powers and to the Avitchi... We must work in the laboratory of the Holy Spirit (sex), in order to transmute our creative power into light and fire. We must cause the energy of the Third Logos to flow inwardly and upwardly, in order to awaken our divine and ineffable creative powers. This is the Magnum Opus!

Fornicators become indigent and miserable shadows... Thereafter, they sink into the frightening Abyss...!

The Seven Words

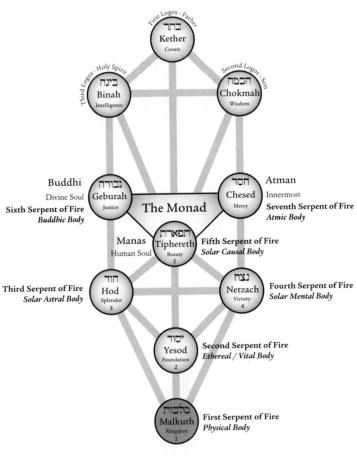

THE TREE OF LIFE AND THE INITIATIONS OF MAJOR MYSTERIES

The Seven Words

When the initiate has made the Kundalini of his Astral Body arrive at the heart, then in the Internal Worlds he experiences the symbolic death and resurrection of our Lord Jesus Christ. Then, in the internal worlds, the initiate lives out the whole drama of Golgotha in his Astral Body. His Judas murders him and a son of Judas stabs the heart of the initiate, with the spear which Longinus wounded the side of the Lord. Then the seven terrific words of Calvary are delivered to the initiate; these words bestow power to the Master over the seven great cosmic planes. These seven words are written with fiery characters on the seven columns of the terribly divine temple of wisdom.

The entire drama of Calvary has to be lived within the Astral plane by means of the third degree of the power of fire.

The seven words correspond to the seven degrees of the power of fire and to the seven tongues of the burning fire of the Dragon of Wisdom.

When the third degree of the power of fire arrives at the heart, the latter shines and becomes resplendent like a Sun of extraordinary beauty.

The third degree of the power of fire totally Christifies the Astral Body and totally opens the chakras of the Astral Body.

The chakras in common and ordinary people are only the senses of their animal-soul. Their chakras are intimately related with the psychic-biological functions of their human organism. The tattvas enter through the chakras and then into our endocrine glands; the endocrine glands then transform the tattvas into hormones.

So, the Astral chakras are the gates of entry for the tattvas.

However when the Astral Body is Christified by means of the third degree of the power of fire, then the seven chakras are transformed into the seven churches to which the Book of Revelation (Apocalypse) refers.

AGNI RIDING UPON THE RAM (LAMB) OF GOD

"Shine thou before us, Agni, well enkindled, with flame, most youthful God, that never fadeth. [...] Seven fuel logs hast thou, seven tongues, O Agni, seven Rishis hast thou, seven beloved mansions. Seven-priests in sevenfold manner pay thee worship. Fill full—All-hail to thee!—seven wombs with butter." - WHITE YAJURVEDA

We stated in our book entitled *The Revolution of Beelzebub* that the seven churches are found located within the Soul-Spirit or Body of the Consciousness, this is how it is; nevertheless, when the third degree of the power of fire opens the Astral chakras, these are then transformed into the very seven churches.

Without the third degree of the power of the fire, the chakras are just purely senses of the animal-soul. Therefore, whosoever is only concerned with the development of the chakras, without working for their Christification, transforms themselves into black magicians.

The God Agni, God of Fire, restores the igneous powers within each of the seven bodies by means of each of the seven great Initiations of Major Mysteries.

Seen clairvoyantly, the God Agni looks like a newborn child; this God is a remarkable majesty of the universe.

Our Astral Body is transformed into a living Nazarene, filled with power and glory when we experience the event of Golgotha in the Astral Body.

This is why we say in our ritual:

> *I believe in the Son, the Cosmic Chrestos, the powerful
> Astral mediation that links our physical personality
> with the supreme immanence of the Solar Father.*

In the Third Initiation of Major Mysteries, the Astral Body passes through the symbolic death and resurrection of the Divine Rabbi of Galilee.

Then, clairvoyantly, we see the Son of Man, our Chrestos, on his cross and thereafter, within his holy sepulcher of glass, before the resurrection.

The initiate is then approved by a sidereal power, and the black magicians, full of anger, attack the initiate incessantly. The seven words then make the initiate omnipotent and powerful.

The occult name of the Astral Body is Zaphnath-Panneah.

The name of the Astral Body is made up of compound names. The first is Zaphnath; this mantra corresponds to our inferior Astral; and the second word, Paaneah, is the Son, our Cosmic Chrestos, which links our physical personality with the supreme immanence of the Solar Father.

Our disciples must acquire the power of Astral Body projection. This power is acquired by vocalizing daily for an hour the sacred mantra *Egipto*. The vowel "E" makes the thyroid gland vibrate and grants the initiate the power of the occult ear. The "G" awakens the chakra of the liver, and when this chakra has reached its full development, then, the initiate can enter and leave the physical body any time at will. The vowel "I," combined with the letter "P," develops clairvoyance in the initiate, and the power to depart in the Astral Body through the window of Brahma, which is the pineal gland. Pronounce the letter "T" with force over the vowel "O," which is intimately related with the chakra of the heart; this is how the initiate can acquire the power to project the self through this plexus and thus travel in his Astral Body.

The correct pronunciation of this mantra is as follows:

Eeeeeeggggggggiiiiiiiipppppppptttooooooo

Those who still do not have the ability to project themselves in the Astral Body with our clues, lack this power. Therefore, they must first acquire it by vocalizing daily for one hour the mantra *Egipto*. This mantra develops the chakras related with the projection of the Astral Body completely. This is how the disciple acquires the power of entering and leaving the physical body at will. Once the power for astral projection is acquired, the disciple will enter and leave the physical body at will.

The Egyptian mantra that is used in order to project oneself in the Astral Body is the following: *Faraon*. This mantra is vocalized during those moments of transition between vigil and sleep, having the mind focused on the pyramids of Egypt.

The correct pronunciation of this mantra is as follows:

Faaaaaaaarrrrrraaaaaeoooooonnnnnnnnnn

This mantra is for Astral Body projections, and as we already stated, it must be pronounced during the states of transition between vigil and sleep, concentrating the mind on the pyramids of Egypt.

However, as we have already stated, the disciples that do not have the power of Astral Body projection must first acquire it, by vocalizing the mantra Egipto for one hour daily.

The death, burial, and resurrection of our Chrestos is accomplished within us by means of the Third Initiation of Major Mysteries.

That is, on the third day, our Cosmic Chrestos, our Astral Body rises from its crystal tomb (Holy Sepulcher). The resurrection and solemn feast is then attained in the superior worlds of consciousness.

The Inner Master attends his solemn feast without material vehicles of any kind.

> *Death is swallowed up in victory. Oh death, where is thy sting? Oh grave, where is thy victory?* - 1 Corinthians 15:54, 55

The mantra **Ephraim** has the power to develop all the chakras and powers of our Cosmic Chrestos.

This mantra is pronounced as follows:

Eeeeeeppphhhrrrrrraaaaauiiiiiimmmmm

All the occult powers of the Astral Body enter into activity with this powerful Egyptian mantra.

The vowel "H" is pronounced like a deep sigh, and the pronunciation of the letter "P" gives force to this vowel like when one is blowing out air.

A catholic priest asked an Aztec magician, "How do you name God?" And the Aztec magician answered him with a deep sigh. This sigh was the vowel "H," this is why the word 'breath' has the vowel "H."

The letter "H" is a vowel, even when the grammarians do not affirm it is. The "H" is the breath of life, the igneous breath, and when combined with the "P," like this, "PH," it gives the sensation of pressuring with the lips, the breath of life.

Thus, this is why this mantra contains remarkable powers.

The vowel "E" develops the thyroid chakra and the powers of the mind. The sound "PH" places the igneous breath on all the chakras of the Astral Body in order to awaken them. The mantra "RA" forces all the chakras of the Astral Body of the human being to vibrate.

The vowel "I" awakens the chakras of the head, and when it is combined with the vowel "M," namely: "IM," it acquires a remarkable power that diffuses through all the astral chakras, by animating and enlightening them.

The vowel "M" is pronounced as a sound that is felt in the mouth, but since the lips are closed, the sound has to come out through the nose. The vowel "M" contains remarkable powers.

The entire secret of the resurrection of our Chrestos resides in the silver cup of Benjamin.

The Nazarenes had a chalice as a sacred symbol.

"They drank from this chalice the semen of Benjamin that was a mixture of wine and water."

Benjamin is a symbol that represents the very essence of our Astral vehicle; properly, such an essence is our Chrestos, who has to pass through the symbolic death of our Lord Jesus Christ. The silver cup found in the sack of Benjamin is our Holy Grail, our divine chalice, filled with seminal energy, filled with the wine of light or the redeeming blood. We achieve the resurrection of our Chrestos by drinking from the chalice of Benjamin.

By performing an in-depth examination on the resurrection of our Chrestos or the Astral Mediator, we can clairvoyantly see an essential depth, a psychic principle, an independent principle, a Superior Astral, represented by Benjamin, the beloved brother of Joseph, son of Jacob.

This divine Astral Body remains for three days within his crystal tomb or Holy Sepulcher. On the third day, this Superior Astral unites or fuses with the Innermost and thus he rises from his tomb. All of this is the initiatic process of the Third Initiation of Major Mysteries.

Within the legend of Joseph, son of Jacob, is enclosed the initiatic process of our Chrestos.

Joseph represents the Astral Body of the Human Being and Benjamin represents the Superior Astral, the Divine Chrestos, which is contained within the Astral Body of the human being (as the silver cup is contained within the sack of Benjamin). Properly stated, the sack is the Astral Body, and the Divine Astral or Benjamin is our Chrestos, who is Benjamin himself, the Superior Astral.

And it is by means of this Divine or Superior Astral that we return to our Father. Joseph saw his father Jacob again by means of Benjamin.

If we observe a wheat spike, we see how it grows, millimeter by millimeter, under the potent rays of the Sun, until it yields the grain; once the grain is yielded, everything else dies.

The chalice of our sexual energy is found within our Astral Body, in other words, within our sack of Benjamin is the chalice whose power creates a type of independent and Superior Astral, which after three days in the resurrection is united and fused with the Innermost.

Properly, this new Astral becomes our Chrestos, who abandons the sack of Benjamin. As the butterfly escapes from its chrysalis, likewise, the new Astral escapes from the Astral "sack" within which he was formed, and exclaims: It is written, I will dwell among your loins.

Life feeds with death and death works for life; our old passions die so that life can surge forth.

This new Astral is an ineffable pleroma, it is an aroma filled with perfections, it is the summum of wisdom.

Theosophists, Rosicrucians, and Spiritualists talk a lot about the Astral Body and think that they know it thoroughly.

But who among them has ever spoken about the third igneous serpent, and about the ultrabiology and ultraphysiology of the Superior Astral? Who among them knew that within the Astral Body another Superior Astral Body is formed? Who among these brothers perhaps knows the manner in which our third serpent ascends through the very subtle medulla of our Benjamin or Superior Astral?

I bluntly affirm that all the books which have been written in the world about Theosophism, Rosicrucianism, Spiritualism, etc., are completely antiquated for the new Aquarian Era, and therefore they must be revised in order to extract from them only what is essential.

Here, I, Samael Aun Weor, deliver unto humanity the authentic message that the White Lodge sends to humanity for the new Aquarian Era.

God has delivered unto humans the wisdom of the serpent. What else do they want? This science is not mine; this science is of God; my person is not worth anything; the work is everything, I am nothing but an emissary.

Not all people have the Superior Astral; such Astral has to be engendered and that Astral is engendered practicing Sexual Magic intensely with the spouse. This is what is called forming the Christ within us. Based on this, the Gnostics affirm that there exist two types of birth: "The birth of the flesh, originated from the coitus, and another different one, for which the coitus is not necessary." From the first type of birth, that is, from the coitus of fornicators, come forth people condemned to death, and from the second type of birth, that is, from sexual magic or conception of the Holy Spirit, Angels come forth, our Chrestos comes forth, the new Astral Body or Mediator Christ comes forth.

Therefore, the path of the domestic home, lived with wisdom and love, leads us to the ineffable joy of Nirvana.

The woman is the path; the woman is the door.

After the resurrection of our Chrestos, the Initiate has to descend into the submerged worlds of the secret enemy.

It is stated that after the resurrection, Christ had to descend into hell in order to take out the souls of our first parents: Abraham, Jacob, etc. from there. This is a living symbol of what the Initiate has to live after his resurrection.

It is unfortunate that the Lutheran Bible has suppressed these Biblical passages written in the original text, and there is no doubt that this is due to the very ignorance of the Protestant sects. Even when the Protestants assure us that Luther did the translation from the authentic original Greek, this is not so, because Martin Luther did not know Greek.

Only we, the Gnostics, possess the original Greek texts of the sacred scriptures, within our holy Gnostic Church. The Bible is the sacred book of the Gnostics, and only the Gnostics can understand it.

The Lutheran Bible is based on the works of St. Jerome, which are intentionally defective, since St. Jerome had to channel things according to the interests of Roman Catholicism (according to the orders received from Pope Danasos). St. Jerome was the true author of the Latin Vulgate.

Therefore, before the ascension, Christ appeared many times to his disciples. When he appeared to the holy women, Christ said unto them:

> *Touch me not; for I am not yet ascended to my Father:*
> *but go to my brethren, and say unto them, I ascend*
> *unto my Father, and your Father, and to my God,*
> *and your God.* - St. John 20:17

This is how, before the ascension, the Initiate has to descend to the submerged worlds in order to destroy the most intimate roots of evil.

Thus, the Initiate penetrates into truly infernal regions, impossible to describe with words.

The ascension comes precisely forty days after the resurrection of our Chrestos.

It would be very difficult to bring the memory of the superior worlds of consciousness into the physical world without the intervention of our Astral Body. The Astral Body is our mediator and as we have already stated, it is intimately related with our endocrine glands and with our grand sympathetic nervous system.

Each of the senses of the Astral Body is found intimately related with the endocrine glands, and because of this it is of indispensable urgency to uproot the Astral Body from the submerged worlds and to make it take root in the plane of the Gods, because the Astral is the instrument which we possess in order to link our earthly personality with the Heavenly Man.

Only in this manner can we explain in what form and in what manner the illumination of the Holy Spirit comes forth after the ascension. Let us read these Biblical verses:

> *But ye shall receive power, after that the Holy Ghost is come upon you: and ye shall be witnesses unto me both in Jerusalem, and in all Judea, and in Samaria, and unto the uttermost part of the earth.*

> *And when he had spoken these things, while they beheld, he was taken up; and a cloud received him out of their sight.* - Acts 1:8, 9

In the Second Initiation of Major Mysteries, we are baptized with water, and in the Third Initiation of Major Mysteries, we are baptized with the fire of the Holy Spirit. John baptized us with water, Christ baptizes us with Fire.

> *For John truly baptized with water; but ye shall be baptized with the Holy Ghost not many days hence.*
> - Acts 1:5

During these forty days that precede the ascension, the Initiate is totally prohibited from all sexual contact, since he must maintain his aura totally luminous and serene, free of any passionate wave.

Only after the forty days, can the Initiate continue practicing his rite of Sexual Magic. But during those forty days preceding the ascension, the Initiate must transmute his sexual energy through the mind. During these forty days preceding the ascension of our Astral Body, we have to inevitably descend into the Abyss in order to definitively cut off all relationships, all roots, all ties with the creatures of evil.

There we meet our former colleagues of evil, and there they ridicule us and attack us incessantly. There we have to live, or better said, relive all those tenebrous scenes of the past, and in this way we cut off the roots that unite the tree of our life to the abysses of evil. Now the Initiate will comprehend why the Master must abstain from the sexual rite with his spouse for those forty days. It is necessary that the aura be brilliant and luminous in order to defend oneself from the potencies of evil, and in order to make it easier for the Hierarchies to do the work of uprooting our Astral vehicle from the putrescence of evil.

This labor is very heavy for the Hierarchies.

Now the devotee of the path will comprehend the eso-teric meaning of Lent. The authentic Lent is not before the Crucifixion of the Master, but after his Crucifixion. But already the Catholic Church and the other Neo-Catholic, Protestant, Adventist sects, etc., lost the tradition of all of this.

It hurts to see how human beings are profoundly rooted in the abyss of evil. In these submerged worlds, painful scenes of the past surge forth before the Initiate, which he has to once again relive in the abyss in order to break every tie with the darkness. This is the farewell that the Initiate bids to darkness.

During this Holy Lent, the Initiate, while not being a demon, is surrounded by demons. This is why, when Mary Magdalene, after exclaiming, "Rabbi, Rabbi!" wanted to touch the Master, Christ said to her:

> *Touch me not; for I am not yet ascended to my Father:*
> *but go to my brethren, and say unto them, I ascend*
> *unto my Father, and your Father; and to my God,*
> *and your God.* - St. John 20:17

Therefore, Christ said to Mary Magdalene, "Do not touch me," because the Astral Body of the Master was surrounded by demons.

Mary Magdalene remarkably loved the Divine Rabbi of Galilee, thus, when she, standing, leaning against a wall, heard the terrible word, "Tibo, Tibo, Tibo!" which condemned the

Christ to pass through the event of Golgotha, she was filled with indescribable terror.

The mission of Christ is indeed terrifying. The Lord loaded upon his shoulders all the weight of a very heavy cross.

The Christic force is what redeems us; the blood of the Lamb is the blood that saves us from the abysses of evil. The doctrine of the resurrection of the dead is the doctrine of Christ.

During this Lent, the Initiate forever breaks those ties that bind the ship of his life to the port of Aeodon (affliction).

In this book, we have talked exclusively about the resurrection and ascension of our Astral Body or Mediator Chrestos: this is the Doctrine of the Nazarene.

In *The Revolution of Beelzebub*, we speak about the resurrection of our Divine Consciousness (High Initiation), and we also speak in that book about that transcendental ascension (which the Nirvani without residues performs, when it fuses with the Glorian).

But now, in this chapter, we will only draw attention to the death, resurrection, and ascension of our Astral Body or Mediator Chrestos.

The entire initiatic process of the Astral Body is found wisely enclosed within the symbolic narration of Joseph, son of Jacob.

Joseph represents the Astral Body of the human being, and Jacob represents the Father, who is in heaven, the Father Star.

Joseph is sold by his own brothers. All our former companions betray us, sell us, when we resolve to tread the rocky path that leads us to Nirvana.

Joseph becomes the servant of a eunuch, and Christ stated: "There be eunuchs, which have made themselves eunuchs for the Kingdom of Heaven's sake." [Matthew 19:12]

When Joseph resolves to follow the path of chastity, he is tempted by a woman and goes to the jail of bitterness, slandered and defamed, but faithful to his pledge of chastity.

And in the prison of pain, we have no consolation other than the bread and the wine of the Transubstantiation. Christ is the cupbearer and baker.

There, it is only the cupbearer and the baker who suffer for us, that is to say, our redeeming Christic substance which redeems us and frees us from the prison of pain and bitterness, until it brings us before the feet of our internal Pharaoh, our sacred Innermost, our King, who makes us masters and lords of the entire land of Egypt.

This is how we attain the High Initiation and prepare ourselves for the resurrection of our Mediating Chrestos. The twelve sons of Jacob, in other words, the Zodiac (the twelve zodiacal constellations), fashion and transform us, until we find our Benjamin, through whom we resurrect and embrace our sidereal Father once again.

We have already explained in our previous books that the Innermost of each human being is a flame that was detached from the consciousness of a sidereal Genie, who is our Father who is in Heaven, the Father of our Innermost, our Jacob.

The Pharaoh's dream is also highly symbolic; the seven years of abundance and the seven years of famine symbolize the seven degrees of the power of the fire, the seven Initiations of Major Mysteries and the bitterness of the seven great Initiations of Major Mysteries, the pains of each of the seven portals.

The silver cup of Benjamin is the semen through which our Astral Body resurrects among the dead.

Joseph's wife Asenath is the Christ-Mind of the Arhat, she is the beautiful Helen, to whom Homer sang his *Iliad*, she is the daughter of the Priest of On, our Innermost, our true Being.

The sons of Joseph are Manasseh and Ephraim. Manases is a tenebrous mantra, within which are enclosed all those forces of evil which removed us from the house of our Father, and which took us out of Eden.

Ephraim is that powerful mantra which makes us fertile in the land of affliction, because it awakens all the powers of our

Astral Body, and because it contains all the divine forces which allow us to return to Eden.

Our Joseph, in other words, our Astral Body, must become free from its imprisonment within corruption so that the resplendent star of Jacob can shine upon his head.

When the Astral Body is liberated from the Abyss, it returns to the star of his Father, which has always smiled upon him; in other words, the Astral Body of the Initiate enters into the stellar aura of his Father.

> *Benjamin shall ravin as a wolf: in the morning he shall devour the prey, and at night he shall divide the spoil.* - Genesis 49:27

Our Benjamin snatches us from the abyss of evil; in the morning he devours the prey of the light, and at night he divides the spoils, when he uproots our Astral Body from the abysses of evil.

> *Joseph is a fruitful bough (the Astral body), even a fruitful bough by a well; whose branches run over the wall.*
>
> *The archers have sorely grieved him, and shot at him and hated him:*
>
> *But his bow abode in strength, and the arms of his hands were made strong by the hands of the mighty God of Jacob (from thence is the shepherd, the stone of Israel),*
>
> *Even by the God of thy Father (the Father Star of the Inner Self), who shall help thee; and by the Almighty, who shall bless thee with blessings of heaven above, blessings of the deep that lieth under, blessings of the breasts, and of the womb:*
>
> *The blessings of thy Father have prevailed above the blessings of thy progenitors unto the utmost bound of the everlasting hills, they shall be on the head of Joseph, and on the crown of the head of him that was separate from his brethren (our Benjamin, who snatches us for God and for the Father).* - Genesis 49:22-26

I do not mean to affirm that Joseph, the patriarch of Egypt did not exist; what I want to affirm is that the drama of Initiation is enclosed within the life of every Initiate.

Likewise, I am not denying the seven years of abundance and famine in Egypt, in accordance with the wise dream of the Pharaoh, which Joseph interpreted. There is no doubt that this occurred; but within all this is contained the Initiatic drama of an Initiate.

The twelve sons of Jacob are merely the twelve zodiacal constellations, within which we have been evolving and devolving.

Therefore, great cosmic truths were left contained within every ancient fable.

The life of every Initiate was written related to purely symbolic figures, and it is only among Initiates that we can understand each other correctly.

Initiation is life itself; therefore, the life of an Initiate correlates to the same drama of Initiation.

Let us look at the following verses:

> And Joseph was brought down to Egypt; and Potiphar, an officer of Pharaoh, captain of the guard, and Egyptian, bought him of the hands of the Ishmeelites, which had brought him down thither.
>
> And it came to pass after these things, that his Master's wife cast her eyes upon Joseph; and she said, Lie with me.
>
> But he refused, and said unto his master's wife, Behold, my master wotteth not what is with me in the house, and he hath committed all that he hath to my hand. - Genesis 39:1, 7, and 8

These verses are a purely allegorical narration; for it is completely impossible for an eunuch, someone who is castrated, to have a woman. That is why, in order to understand the Bible, one needs to be a Gnostic, because the Bible is a highly symbolic book, and if we try to read it in the Protestant style, like one who reads newspaper columns, we fall into the most terrible absurdities.

The entire story of Joseph is a sacred chest within which the very drama of Calvary is enclosed. In order to understand the symbolic story of Joseph, the Patriarch, one needs to be an Initiate.

The third chapter of Genesis shows us how and in what manner man came out of Eden; this is why the chapters that deal with the story of Joseph are in the same Genesis, because they explain to us how the human being came out of the house of his Father, and how, and in what manner, the human being can return to the arms of his Father, and to the ineffable bliss of Eden, to the paradise, out of which he came.

The resurrection of the Son of Man is only possible by drinking from Benjamin's silver cup, in other words, is only possible by the man practicing Sexual Magic intensely with the woman.

Benjamin snatches us for God and for the Father.

The narration of Joseph encloses the secret to return to Eden, and this is why such a narration is found written in the same Genesis.

The woman tempts Joseph, and Joseph overcomes the temptation: this encloses the clue to Sexual Magic. Whosoever has ears, let him hear, and whosoever has understanding, let him understand, for there is wisdom within.

During this Holy Lent that precedes the ascension of the Master, the ineffable verb of the great enlightened beings resounds with a mysterious echo within the closed temple. These are forty days of terrible efforts for the Sacred College of Initiates.

Thus, the Masters, by singing mysterious songs in a sacred language within the closed temple, detach with the power of their sacred verb, our Astral vehicle from the profound roots of the evilness of the Abyss, within which our Astral Body is rooted since ancient times.

There we must live, or better said, experience again all the tenebrous scenes of the past, like bidding a last farewell to the darkness.

It is a law of Nature to recapitulate past events before initiating new manifestations. This is why before its birth, the human fetus recapitulates within the womb all the past processes of human evolution.

Before initiating the Age of the Rainbow, our chemical Earth recapitulated the Lunar, Solar, and Saturnian periods.

Therefore, before his ascension, the Initiate after his resurrection must recapitulate his entire past within the abyss.

The Initiate begins recapitulating the most tenebrous scenes of his past within truly infernal spheres; thereafter little by little he ascends to less terrible spheres and less barbarous scenes.

In the abyss, we experience again all the terrible evils of our past incarnations; here is where we realize what Christ means to us.

Indeed, it would be impossible to come out from within the abyss without the help of the divine Savior of the World.

The doctrine of the resurrection of the dead is the doctrine of Christ.

Dead are all human beings, and only by means of the blood of the Martyr of Golgotha will all human beings be able to resurrect.

When the Human Soul resurrects from among the living dead, the soul then becomes an Angel, unto whom all the marvels and powers of the subtle worlds are disclosed; thus, all the veils are lifted for the Initiate, who is transformed into a God of the universe.

This is the doctrine that Christ taught secretly to his seventy disciples.

> Now if Christ be preached that he rose from the dead,
> how say some among you that there is no resurrection
> of the dead?

But if there be no resurrection of the dead, then is Christ not risen.

And if Christ be not risen, then is our preaching vain, and your Faith is also vain.

Yea, and we are found false witnesses of God; because we have testified of God that he raised up Christ: whom he raised not up, if so be that the dead rise not.

For if the dead rise not, then is Christ not raised.

And if Christ be not raised, your faith is vain; ye are yet in your sins.

Then they also which are fallen asleep in Christ are perished.

If in this life only we have hope in Christ, we are of all men most miserable.

But now is Christ risen from the dead, and become the first fruits of them that slept.

For since by man came death, by man came also the resurrection of the dead.

For as in Adam all die, even so in Christ shall all be made alive. - 1 Corinthians 15:12-22

Therefore the doctrine of Christ is the doctrine of the resurrection of the dead.

We, Gnostics, understand as "dead" the living dead, in other words, the entire humanity.

We call all human beings "the living dead" because of the following reasons:

1. They do not see, nor hear anything of what occurs in the Internal Worlds.
2. They are subject to illnesses and death.
3. They do not know how to handle the universal forces.
4. They are subject to pain and bitterness.
5. They do not have power over the mysteries of life and death nor do they know them.

6. They die against their will and are born against their will; they do not know how they are born or die.

7. They are inhabitants of the abyss.

Now then, we, Gnostics, teach that the resurrection of the dead is only attainable by means of Initiation.

The resurrection of the dead is performed on the soul and not on the physical body.

> *Now this I say, brethren, that flesh and blood cannot inherit the kingdom of God; neither doth corruption inherit incorruption.* - 1 Corinthians 15: 50
>
> *So also is the resurrection of the dead. It is sown in corruption; it is raised in incorruption:*
>
> *It is sown in dishonor; it is raised in glory: it is sown in weakness; it is raised in power:*
>
> *It is sown a natural body; it is raised a spiritual body. There is a natural body, and there is a spiritual body.*
>
> *And so it is written, the first man Adam was made a living soul; the last Adam was made a quickening spirit.*
>
> *Howbeit that was not first which is spiritual, but that which is natural; and afterward that which is spiritual.*
>
> *The first man is of the earth, earthy: the second man is the Lord from heaven.* - 1 Corinthians 15: 42-47

The former verses completely demonstrate that the resurrection of the dead pertains to the soul and not to the physical body.

It would be absolutely ludicrous and completely laughable to believe that in order to resuscitate at the end of the sound of the great trumpet (within the grave) the bones will join the bones, such as Protestants, Catholics, Adventists, Presbyterians, etc., naively believe. Only those who do not possess divine understanding can accept such an absurdity.

Therefore, the resurrection of the dead is only attainable by means of the occult wisdom!

*But we speak the wisdom of God in a mystery, even
the occult wisdom which God ordained before the
world unto our glory.* - 1 Corinthians 2:7

A child of resurrection has the following powers:

1. He has the power to see and hear in all the internal worlds.

2. He has the power to manipulate the mysteries of life and death.

3. He is given power to judge the living dead (the entire humanity).

4. One is born at will and disembodies at will.

5. One has the power to calm tempests or to unleash them, at will.

6. Powers to make the earth tremble and to sink continents at will.

7. Powers over fire and hurricanes, etc.

Sanat Kumara, the Ancient of the Days and Lord of the World, was the founder of the College of Initiates of the great, universal White Fraternity. This great Being is one of the Four Thrones of whom the Holy Bible speaks. He has been living in Asia for many millions of years with the same physical body that he brought to the Earth since the times of Lemuria. Death has not and shall never have power over him, because he is a child of resurrection, and death has no power over any child of resurrection.

Master Morya, Master of the ray of Mars, dwells in the Himalayas, at the edge of a road. He dwells in a humble house; he has innumerable disciples, and his present body has an age of more than nine hundred years. Against Master Morya, death has not and shall not succeed either, because Master Morya is a child of the resurrection of the dead, and death cannot succeed over any son of resurrection.

Death only has power over the weak, over cowards, over the living dead, over the children of the Great Whore who have been incapable, who have not had the courage to put an end to their filthy fornication.

Master Kout-Humi is also well known in the West and belongs to the ray of wisdom. He is also of an indecipherable age, and has his sanctuary on the snowy peaks of the Himalayas. He is another child of the resurrection, and death has not succeeded over him, because death only has power over fools, over fornicators and adulterers.

Master D. K. (Djwal Khul) is another child of resurrection, another Superman who has known how to take advantage of his sexual energy. This Master belongs to the ray of Mercury; he helped Master H. P. Blavatsky, by dictating to her a great part of *The Secret Doctrine*.

He presently possesses the same physical body that he had in the year 1675, and death has not had power over him because he is a child of the resurrection.

Let us now mention Paul of Tarsus. This Master is presently incarnated and is Master Hilarion. Such a Master is the author of the book entitled *Light on the Path*. Master Hilarion unfolds in the ray of science. He is a Master of the ray of Mercury.

Master Serapis, Master of the ray of Venus, is another child of resurrection. He is of an incalculable age; he directs the world art.

Master Rakoczi is the same Count Saint Germain, Roger Bacon, and Francis Bacon. This Master directs world politics. He presently lives in Tibet, and possesses the same physical body with which he was known during the seventeenth, eighteenth, and nineteenth centuries in all the courts of Europe. The centuries have passed over this Master without death having any power over him, because he is a child of resurrection. This Master is of the ray of Jupiter.

Each of these Masters belongs to a certain ray, for there are seven rays of cosmic evolution:

1. The Lunar ray
2. The Mercurian ray

3. The Venusian ray

4. The Solar ray

5. The Martian ray

6. The Jupiterian ray

7. The Saturnian ray

What Theosophists state about Initiates entering another cosmic ray in each Initiation of Major Mysteries is not true.

Each Master evolves and unfolds in his own ray, and never changes rays. In the internal worlds, each of the seven rays has its temple of mysteries.

I, Samael Aun Weor, Master of the ray of Mars, give testimony to these things, not because I have read it through books (as is done by those who theorize), but because I have lived it. I am a child of the resurrection, and I give testimony of the resurrection of the dead, because I, Aun Weor, resurrected among the living dead, and my duty as Initiator of the new Age of Aquarius is to give testimony of the holy doctrine of the divine Rabbi of Galilee, so that this holy doctrine of the Savior of the World is spread over the entire face of the earth without distinctions of race, sex, caste, or color.

Each of these rays has its chief:

1. Chief of the Lunar ray: Gabriel

2. Chief of the Mercurian ray: Raphael

3. Chief of the Venusian ray: Uriel

4. Chief of the Solar ray: Michael

5. Chief of the Martian ray: Samael

6. Chief of the Jupiterian ray: Zachariel

7. Chief of the Saturnian ray: Orifiel

These are the seven rays of which the Theosophists have spoken so much and to which they have dedicated entire volumes, without ever having given the exact and concrete explanation about them. The Theosophists have described the rays in such a nebulous and vague manner that they really do not meet the inner aspirations of the soul. Indeed,

Theosophists need to become practitioners; the teachings of the Theosophical Society are useless to anyone because they lack practice.

Every human being can know to what ray he belongs by merely counting the transverse lines on his forehead.

Those who have a single line belong to the Lunar ray.

Those who have two lines belong to the Mercurian ray.

Those who have three lines belong to the Venusian ray.

Those who have four lines belong to the Solar ray.

Those who have five lines belong to the Martian ray.

Those who have six lines belong to the Jupiterian ray.

Those who have seven lines belong to the Saturnian ray (read *Zodiacal Course* by the same author).

All of us, the Masters of the Seven Rays, are "children of the resurrection," and we have all gone through the bitterness of Calvary; we have all experienced within ourselves the ascension of the Lord.

No Master ever leaves his ray; each Master works only in his ray. The chief of our ray is our Father, who is in Heaven. No Master ever abandons his Father who is in Heaven; that is why it is impossible for a Master to go from one ray to another, as the Theosophists believe.

I, Aun Weor, am the son of my Father Samael, and even when in my past I evolved under the rulership of different planets, I was never able to leave the ray of Samael, because Aun Weor is a spark emanated from the flame of Samael; therefore, I came from Samael, and I returned to Samael. Thus, I have always had five lines on my forehead in all my reincarnations.

In the ascension of the Lord, our Astral Body becomes liberated from the abyss and ascends within the luminous aura of our Father, who is in Heaven.

As if descending from the blue of infinity, Sanat Kumara (in whose name all Initiations are received) appears radiantly upon the holy altar when the inner Master kneeling before the sacred altar of the Third Initiation of Major Mysteries receives his Initiation.

The sublime presence of this Ancient of the Days is indescribable.

His grey hair (that seems to have never been touched by scissors) falls over his shoulders. His white beard and majestic face reveal to us the likeness of God.

Sanat Kumara with his semi-nude body, holding a staff with his hand, resembles an Adamite.

Sanat Kumara is the outcome of millenary purifications.

The Third Initiation of Major Mysteries is received by the Inner Master within the superior worlds of consciousness, and he attends his Initiation without material bodies of any kind.

This ancient doctrine of initiatic resurrection was known by all the Gnostic sects of olden times, by all the initiatic societies of the past: Nazarenes, Peratae, Pythagoreans, etc. The resurrection was cultivated in the mysteries of Egypt, Greece, Rome, Babylon, Syria, India, Mexico, Peru, Troy, Carthage, etc.

The resurrection was the doctrine of the Essenes; the resurrection was the doctrine of the sages of the past; this is the wisdom of the Gnostics.

Isis always lives resurrecting Osiris by means of the sacred phallus.

The wisdom of sex is the foundation of every authentic school of mysteries. This is the Lingam-Yoni of the Greek mysteries.

Redemption resides exclusively in Sexual Magic.

By means of Sexual Magic and perfect sanctity, everyone can become a Master of Major Mysteries of the great, universal White Fraternity.

The scientific process of ascension produces in the body of the Initiate a process of biological transformation, whose symptoms express themselves in the form of decline or organic weakness, especially when the hour of dusk arrives.

However, that does not mean illness or organic weakness as such, but simply, fleeting phenomena, which are the outcome of the transformation of the Astral Body during those forty days of the ascension of the Lord.

It is logical that every transformation of the Astral Body originates a similar transformation in the catalytic cellular processes, and in the electro-biological mechanism of our endocrine glands, which like marvelous laboratories transform the tattvas into different biochemical substances, whose most diverse combinations, in the end, define themselves as hormones.

The Astral Body has its seat in the liver. If we examine the word "higado" [Editor's note: the Spanish word for liver], we see that it has three letters: I, A, O. Diodorus stated in one of his verses: "Know that among all the Gods, the most elevated is IAO. Hades is in the winter. Zeus begins in spring, Helios in summer, and in autumn, IAO enters into activity, working constantly. IAO is Jovis-Pater; he is Jupiter, who is unjustly called Javhe by the Jews. IAO offers the substantial wine of life, while Jupiter is a slave of the Sun." (Page 97, *The Gnostic Church*, by Huiracocha, fourth edition.)

It is necessary to detach the Astral Body from the infernos of the human being.

In the esoteric chamber related with the zodiacal sign of Virgo, we are taught that the roots of the very tree of existence reside in the womb. An in-depth examination of the intestines permits us to corroborate this affirmation. Observe the curious analogy that exists between the roots of trees and the roots of the tree of our own life. These roots are our intestines, so intimately related with the zodiacal sign of Virgo.

Just as the roots of trees absorb their life from the clay of the earth in order to transform it into nutritional sap, which spreads through all the veins and cells of the tree, likewise our intestinal roots wisely extract from food, the most diverse vital principles, to nourish with them, the marvelous tree of our own organic biology.

Just as the clay of the earth is found at the profound seat of the roots of the trees, likewise in the profound seats of our lower abdomen and of our liver (like strata, spheres or submerged worlds constituted by the atoms of the secret enemy) the infernos of the human being are found.

During these forty days of the ascension of the Lord, the creative Hierarchies have to detach our Astral Body from these infernos of the human being, where we experience again and recapitulate all the tenebrous scenes of the past.

That recapitulation begins after the resurrection of our Chrestos.

This recapitulative process is initiated beginning with the most tenebrous submerged sphere of the universe, which is bloody red in color, and in whose horrible abysses live all the monsters and evils of the world.

Thereafter, by recapitulating all our tenebrous scenes, we ascend little by little through different strata, regions or planes of the atoms of the secret enemy.

Nineteen days after the resurrection of our Chrestos, a certain layer of atomic substance of the Astral counterpart of our abdomen is torn away by the Hierarchies.

Such a layer, similar to the skin of our human organism, is like the door to the infernos of the human being, formed by the atoms of the secret enemy.

This closed door keeps the Human Soul prisoner within the abysses of evil.

Once this thick atomic layer of the Astral counterpart of our abdomen is removed, the Masters then have to medicate this zone of our abdomen.

Naturally, all these diverse transformations of our Astral Body inevitably have repercussions upon our inner organic biology, originating symptoms of fleeting organic weakness and sporadic manifestations of hunger in the physical body of the Master.

If we break up the number nineteen in the following manner: 1 + 9, it gives us the sum of ten.

Now then, the entire progress of the devotee of the path is based on the numbers 1 + 2 + 3 + 4 = 10. Now my disciples will understand why it is that in precisely nineteen days, the atomic door that keeps the Astral Body prisoner within the infernos of man should be torn away.

Naturally, we will explain to our disciples that the state of imprisonment to which we refer, is only referring to the vital essence of our Astral Body; in other words, to the very roots of our marvelous Astral vehicle, enclosed within the profundities of the abyss; these roots are the submerged essence of the very roots of our organic tree. These are the infernos of the human being, from which our Astral Body must be detached. Thus, this is why the entire progress of the student is based on the number ten. The ten Sephiroth of Kabbalah are based on the number ten. These ten Sephiroth are the following:

1. Kether, Wisdom; "The Magician" of the first Arcana of the Tarot, whose primitive hieroglyph is represented by a man.

2. Chokmah, Love; the Empress of the Tarot, the Priestess, the second card of the Tarot; the Moon; primitive hieroglyph, the mouth of man.

3. Binah, Power; planet Venus; third card of the Tarot, the Empress; the primitive symbol is a hand in the attitude of taking.

These three Sephiroth are the Sephirothic Crown.

Then the seven Sephiroth proceed in the following order:

4. Chesed, Jupiter; the Divine Being; Atman; primitive hieroglyph: a breast. The fourth card of the Tarot; Mercy; the plate of the Emperor.

5. Geburah, rigor; the fifth card of man; the Pope or Hierophant of the Tarot; Mars the warrior.

6. Tiphereth, Venus; beauty; love of the Holy Spirit; the Causal Body of man; the sixth card of the Tarot, the Lovers.

7. Netzach, Mercury; the chariot of the Tarot; the seventh card and the eternity of everything.

8. Hod, the Justice of the Arcana; the eighth card of the Tarot, Saturn, victory.

9. Yesod, the Sun; the ninth card of the Tarot, the Hermit, the Absolute.

10. Malkuth, the entire universe; Mary or Virgo; Nature.

These ten Sephiroth live, evolve and progress within the consciousness. The human being is the same Sephirothic tree. It is very interesting that man has ten fingers on his hands, and that the Decalogue is made up of Ten Commandments. Now the devotee of the path will comprehend the importance of the number ten. Now my disciples will understand why nineteen days after the resurrection of our own Chrestos the atomic door is torn away by the Masters from the infernos of the human being.

When Paul of Tarsus wrote his Epistle to the Philippians, he still did not attain the resurrection. Let us look at the following verses, which will prove my affirmation:

> But what things were gain to me, those I counted loss for Christ.
>
> Yea doubtless, and I count all things but loss for the excellency of the knowledge of Christ Jesus my Lord: for whom I have suffered the loss of all things, and do count them but dung, that I may win Christ.
>
> And be found in him, not having mine own righteousness, which is of the law, but that which is through the faith of Christ, the righteousness which is of God by faith:
>
> That I may know him, and the power of his resurrection, and the fellowships of his sufferings, being made comfortable unto his death.
>
> If by any means I might attain unto the resurrection of the dead (Third Initiation of Major Mysteries).
>
> Not as though I had already attained, either were already perfect: but If follow after, if that I may apprehend that for which also I am apprehended of Christ Jesus.

Brethren, I count myself not to have apprehended: but
this one thing I do, forgetting those things which are
behind, and reaching forth unto those things which are
before.

I press towards the mark for the prize of the high
calling of God in Christ Jesus. - Philippians 3:7-14

Nevertheless, Paul has already achieved the resurrection and is presently incarnated once again; he is Master Hilarion, author of the book *Light on the Path.*

This is the doctrine of the first fathers of the Gnostic-Catholic Church. To this doctrine belonged Basilides, Saturnius of Antioch, Simon Magus, Carpocrates, founder of various convents in Spain, Marcion of Pontus, Saint Thomas, Valentinus, St. Augustine, Tertulian, St. Ambrose, Ireneaus, Hyppolitus, Epiphanius, Clement of Alexandria, Marcus, Cerdo, Empedocles, St. Jerome, etc. This is the ancient doctrine of the Nazarenes, of the Sethians, the Peratae, the Valentinians, the Justinians, etc. This is the ancient doctrine which was known in all the ancient schools of mysteries, and which Christ taught in secrecy to his seventy disciples. This is the secret science that I, Samael Aun Weor, am diffusing publicly to initiate the Age of Aquarius. This is the secret doctrine of our Divine Savior; all this Gnostic Wisdom is enclosed within *The Pistis Sophia.*

The book *Pistis Sophia* consists of four parts; the first and fourth parts do not have a title, but the second part of this book has a title that reads: "Part of the volumes of the Savior," and at the beginning of the second book the following inscription is found: "Second book of the Pistis Sophia." This refers to the greatest book of all the Gnostic doctrines, which was published in Latin in the year 1851 by Schwartz and Petermann, according to a codex of the London Museum entitled Askeniean (whose age is dated back to the third century, although some believe that it is of the fifth century, Opus Onosticum Valentinus Adjuticatum est codice manuscripto Coptico Londinense descripsit et latine vertit M. G Schwartze version of *The Gnostic Church* by Krumm-Heller, page 12, Fourth Edition).

Therefore, the esoteric doctrine of the resurrection, as we are teaching it here, is enclosed in the one hundred forty-eight chapters of *The Pistis Sophia,* and in the profound esoteric wisdom of the holy Bible.

It is a pity that Master Blavatsky did not find the Gnostic treasures.

The doctrine of the holy Gnostic Church is the wisdom of our Lord Jesus Christ.

Let us now proceed with epiphany: this old word comes from Greek. Epiphany is the ascension, revelation, or manifestation of Christ in us, after the resurrection of our Chrestos. This ascension takes us to the illumination of the Holy Spirit after having recapitulated our entire past within the profound abyss of evil.

With epiphany we receive illumination, but during the forty days which precede the ascension, we sink into profound darkness.

To reach the very elevated heights of the resurrection appears to be very distant and difficult to many brothers and sisters, but everyone who puts an end to fornication will soon reach those ineffable peaks.

The Bible tells us the following:

> *Marriage is honorable in all, and the bed undefiled:*
> *but whoremongers and adulterers God will judge.-*
> Hebrews 13:4

With this verse, the Bible, which is God's word, teaches us that the redemption of the human being resides exclusively in Sexual Magic, because the undefiled bed, separated from fornication and adultery is only possible by practicing Sexual Magic with one's priestess-spouse, instead of the filthy coition.

> *Lest there be any fornicator, or profane person, as*
> *Esau, who for one morsel of meat sold his birthright. -*
> Hebrews 12:16

And in this manner, following the path of sanctity, we prepare ourselves for epiphany, and we realize in ourselves the Christ-Being.

It is necessary for every Initiate to pray daily to God. Every prayer must be accompanied by a cup of wine and a piece of bread. "Do this in remembrance of me," said our Divine Savior.

The Roman priests monopolized the Holy Unction, and due to this, wretched humanity lost twenty centuries without it.

Brethren of mine, pray always, and thereafter eat the bread and drink the wine. I owe this solemn teaching to the Angel Aroch, Angel of command.

Each person can, while alone, pray and persevere in the partaking of the bread and wine.

The most powerful prayer is the Our Father.

The bread and wine should always be placed on a clean and perfumed cloth. The bread and wine can only be brought to the mouth after praying.

Through the bread and wine, billions of Christic atoms, which come to awaken all our occult powers, enter our human organism.

Christ, in his capacity as the Cosmic Christ, said:

> I am the bread of life, I am the living bread; if anyone eats of this bread, he will live eternally; whoever eats of my flesh and drinks of my blood, he dwells in me and I in him.

Now, with this teaching, every human being will be able to Christify himself by means of Sexual Magic and of the Holy Eucharistic Unction.

All our brethren must always have the bread and wine at hand, and persevere daily in the Holy Unction.

The prayer is always performed on one's knees.

It is necessary to know how to pray: to pray is to converse with God.

When the Angel Aroch, Angel of command, taught me this marvelous clue of the Gnostic Unction, he also taught me how to pray.

Unutterable are those ineffable moments in which the Angel Aroch, in the form of a child, on his knees and with his hands together over his chest, raised his very pure eyes towards heaven. At that instant, his face seemed on fire, and full of profound love, he exclaimed: "Lord, Lord, do not let me fall, do not ever let me leave the light," etc. He then broke the bread and gave us to eat, and he poured into a small silver jug the wine: he served the wine in some cups and gave us to drink.

These Angels no longer use the old Lunar Astral Body; they only use the Superior Astral Body, our Benjamin, and that is why they resemble children of indescribable beauty.

They are the children of the resurrection; these are the children of life, and only terrific lightning emerges from within their foreheads.

With the help of these Angels, one can transport oneself in the "Jinn" state in the body of flesh and bones to the most remote places of the earth. During the state of transition between vigil and sleep, one can invoke any of these Angels, begging them to transport us with the physical body to the place that we wish; and if the Angel considers our petition to be a just one, he will transport us to the desired place: it will be enough to rise from the bed full of faith, but preserving sleepiness. (See Chapter XII of Acts in the New Testament).

The Benjamin of a Master is a precious acquisition; it is sufficient for a Master to think of a specific person or distant place to find himself there in a few instants, seeing and hearing everything that happens.

When the days of the ascension of the Master are already approaching, the latter begins to perceive, in the superior worlds of consciousness where the Light of the Spirit shines, a closed temple whose doors will open after forty days to receive and accept him as an authentic dweller of the ineffable worlds of the pure Spirit, where the ineffable love of the Father shines.

Ecstatic, the internal Master contemplates that sublime ineffable temple, upon whose triangular dome rests the white dove of the Holy Spirit, with his divine likeness of an Elder.

Inside the internal Master, within whom our beloved Benjamin has been totally absorbed, our Divine Consciousness vibrates intensely.

Now then, we must know that between our Divine Consciousness and the old Astral Body, there fortunately exists a terrific ray of the Cosmic Christ, in other words, the third degree of the power of fire, which unites our old Astral Body with our Divine Consciousness.

This Christic Ray is the mediator between the Astral and the internal Master, within which the ineffable life of our Benjamin is agitated.

The Christic Ray, or Kundalini of the Astral Body, is therefore like the sacred hand of the divine Savior of the World, which takes us out of the abyss and tears us away from the darkness forever.

It is like the saving hand of the Master, which extends itself towards us to lift us to the ineffable temple of the Father.

Christ comes to us like a thief in the night, when we least expect him. The awakening of the Kundalini of the Astral Body or Christic Ray is like a terrible ray of lightning. In the beginning, the Astral Kundalini (Ray of Jesus Christ) has a beautiful, resplendent, white color, but when it has reached its total development, it then has a sublime golden color, full of indescribable splendor.

And it is through the third degree of the power of fire how Christ fulfills his word that he pledged in that solemn pact, signed with blood in the event of Golgotha.

When the third degree of the power of the fire manages to come out through the superior part of the cranium, it takes up the mystical shape of a white dove with the head of an Elder:

this is the dove of the Holy Spirit, which remains resting on that triangular dome of that ineffable temple, waiting for the sublime hour, the ineffable moment in which all the lent days of the Master have passed in order for the doors of the temple of the Father to open.

At the door of that majestic temple where the light of the Father shines, two images of our Astral are seen, waiting for the solemn hour in which the doors will open.

Within the abyss, on the thirty-third day of tenebrous recapitulations, our three inferior vehicles, or better said, the psychic consciousness of our three inferior vehicles is examined with fire.

It is necessary to examine these three inferior vehicles in order to know the outcome of these tenebrous recapitulations within the abyss.

Then, a Hierarch casts three loaves of bread on the ground, and these three loaves of bread explode like fiery bombs, and become scorching fire.

And there among the flames of scorching fire, we then see three beautiful maidens resisting the test of fire.

These three maidens are the psychic consciousness and the ethereal principles of our physical, vital, and astral bodies.

If any of these ladies or beautiful youths succumb to the fire, or better said, were to flee or tremble with terror, or faint within the igneous flames, it would have then been verified with this examination that our stone is poorly forged.

In this case, the Master would be postponed, until achieving the polishing of each one of his facets with the hard emery of pain.

Thus, when the diamond of our Soul has already been polished and shines with all of its splendor, it is only then that the Master is totally prepared for the ascension of the Lord.

These three damsels are the Soul of each of our three inferior vehicles.

In order to attain the ascension, we have to extract from each of our three inferior vehicles a pure and beautiful spiritual extract.

These three bodies of sin have to give us a divine triune Soul, for God and for the Father.

This is the mystery of Baphomet.

Our physical, vital, and astral bodies are marvelous.

> *Happy is the man that hath his quiver full of them:*
> *they shall not be ashamed, but they shall speak with*
> *the enemies in the gate.* - Psalm 127:5

In this examination we see a fourth loaf of bread that does not enter the state of ignition, because it symbolizes the Mental Body and the Fourth Initiation of Major Mysteries, to which the Master has access only after the ascension.

When the Master comes out triumphant from this test of the thirty-three days, he is then shown an old defective lamp, which represents our old submerged world, and he is told: "That is no longer good."

The former quoted phrase means that the past has already given its fruits and the false light of the tenebrous Lucifers and the false light of reasoning are no longer good for anything. Now we need a new light, the light of the pure Spirit, the light of Christ, the ineffable light of the Father.

Once the thirty-three days have passed, and after the examination to which the triune Soul of our physical, vital and astral bodies is submitted, the Master acquires terrible powers over the tenebrous forces of the Abyss.

By dominating passionate temptations during this Holy Lent, the Initiate steals from the devil all the powers and becomes omnipotent and powerful.

Then, a transformation in the metallic sound of his voice is produced.

Then, ardent temptations no longer produce within him those states of ardent arousal. He has stolen the fire from the devil, thus, the devil no longer has a Mendes. This is the terrible secret of Baphomet: Light emerges from within the darkness, and the rose, which perfumes the air with its delightful aromas, extracts its marvelous perfume from within the very mud of the earth. The mystery of Baphomet is simply a mystery of Alchemy.

After these thirty-three days, the swollen waves of seductive temptation will in vain knock the steely shield of the warrior with their lust.

The Master has now become of steel, and passions no longer provoke in him the torture of Tantalus, the terrible desire for coition.

Now the Master is a dictator of strength; now the Master is a terrible warrior, because he stole power from the devil, and the frightened darkness flees terrified.

Before, the swollen waves of the Red Sea looked at him with infinite provocation, and the Master suffered the terrible ardor of passionate thirst, against which he valiantly held the sword of will. Now, the swollen waves of the Red Sea look at him terrified, and the darkness, crying, flee terrified.

This is the mystery of the male goat of Mendes. This is the terrible secret of Baphomet.

The feet of the thrones of the Masters are made of monsters, and the sacred objects of the temples are sustained on animal-like pedestals.

Three days before the ascension of the Lord, the Initiate begins to enter regions of ineffable beauty, because Nature does not make any leaps: Natura non facit saltus.

The day is always preceded by the aurora, and a grown-up must first be a child and then an adolescent.

Precisely thirty-seven days later, the Initiate, in his Astral Body, must review the twelve zodiacal constellations, within which he developed and evolved, in an analogous manner to the development and evolution of the fetus within the maternal womb.

The Zodiac is the womb of our solar system and the cosmic womb of our Souls.

Each of the twelve zodiacal constellations has its own color.

The light of Leo has a beautiful golden-yellow color, and the Initiate reviews all the twelve zodiacal constellations in reverse order until he reaches Leo. This constellation governs the heart, which is the temple of the Innermost: Now our disciples will comprehend why we make a complete turn around the Zodiac until we reach Leo.

We are the children of the lords of the flame, whose dwelling is in the constellation of Leo. Our evolution begins and ends in Leo.

Spiritually, each human Spirit has his Father who is in Heaven, but the Lords of the Flame endowed us with a Spiritual Body and a Carnal Body, and it is from this point of view that we are children of the Lords of the Flame.

Light is seminal substance. Thus, the semen of the twelve zodiacal constellations developed us within the uterus of this zodiac.

Light is always accompanied by the luminous verb.

The substratum of the spoken word is the Solar Word. We already know that the Logos sounds. Now then: there are twenty-four vowels that the Initiate sees and hears. These twenty-four vowels correspond to the twelve zodiacal signs.

The twenty-four melodies of the zodiac resound throughout the whole of creation with the entire grandiose euphoria of the Mahamanvantara. That is the Word of God, sustaining the universe firmly on its march. (Read *Logos, Mantra, Magic* by Krumm-Heller (Huiracocha)).

Once the Holy Lent is completed, the ascension of the Lord follows, and the Initiate is then received with a great feast and delightful music in that ineffable temple of the kingdom of the Spirit.

The night of the ascension is very interesting. The house of the Initiate is invaded by millions of black magicians, who, full of anger, try to apprehend the Master, offended to see that one more soul escapes them to head towards the ineffable kingdom of light.

In the temple, the Master must ask for the dove of the Holy Spirit.

> *And I say unto you, Ask, and it shall be given you; seek, and ye shall find; knock, and it shall be opened unto you.*
>
> *For everyone that asketh receiveth; and he that seeketh, findeth; and to him that knocketh it shall be opened.*
>
> *If a son shall ask bread of any of you that is a father, will he give him a stone? Or if he asks for a fish, will he for a fish give him a serpent?*
>
> *Or if he shall ash for an egg, will he offer him a scorpion?*
>
> *If ye then being evil, know how to give good gifts unto your children: how much more shall your Heavenly Father give the Holy Spirit to them that ask him?*
>
> - Luke 11: 9-13

The ascension of the Master is announced by four Angels of the temple, who, facing the four cardinal points of the earth, each blow their trumpet, and then the Son, that is to say, our Astral, is lifted upwards, towards Heaven, and in this manner are fulfilled the holy scriptures, which textually say the following:

> *But ye shall receive power, after that the Holy Ghost is come upon you: and ye shall be witnesses unto me both in Jerusalem, and in all Judea, and in Samaria, and unto the uttermost part of the earth.*
>
> *And when he had spoken these things, while they beheld, he was taken up; and in cloud received him out of their sight.* - The Acts of the Apostles 1:8-9

As of that instant, the Master is received above, in the superior worlds of consciousness, and the seven words of Calvary make him omnipotent and powerful.

> *When the Son of man shall come in his glory, and all the holy Angels with him, then shall he sit upon the throne of his glory.* - St. Matthew 25:31

The Son of Man is our Soul, who now sits upon the throne of glory.

> *To him that overcometh will I grant to sit with me on my throne, even as I also overcame, and am sat down with my Father in his throne.* - Revelation 3:21

The throne of the Innermost is the throne of the Father, thus, whosoever overcomes, sits with the Father on his throne. And in this manner, the word pledged by Christ on Mount Calvary is fulfilled.

Christ came in order to fulfill this, to save humanity, and it is only in this way, in this manner that Christ saves humanity. The Gnostic scriptures state the following:

> *And Jesus, the divine great Gnostic priest, intoned a sweet hymn in praise of the great Name and said to his disciples: Come unto me! And they did so. Then he addressed the four cardinal points, extended his quiet look and pronounced the profoundly sacred name: JEU; and he blessed them and blew in their eyes.*

> *Look above! he exclaimed. Thou art now clairvoyant.*

> *They then lifted their eyes to where Jesus was pointing and they saw a great Light that no human being could describe.*

> *And the great priest said: Look away from that great Light and look towards the other side. They then saw a great Fire, Water, Wine, and Blood.*

> *And he continued: Truly I tell thee that I have brought nothing to this world but Fire, Water, Wine, and the Blood of Redemption. I have brought Fire and Water from the place of the Light, from there where the Light is found. And I have brought the Wine and Blood from the dwelling of Barbelo. After some time has passed, the Father has sent me to the Holy Spirit in the form of a White Dove. But listen: the Fire, the Water, and the Wine are for the purification and the forgiveness of sins. The Blood that was given to me as*

a symbol of the human body, I received in the dwelling of Barbelo, of the great strength of the Universal God.

The Holy Spirit, as in me, descends, and will take everyone to the Supreme Place of the Light. That is why I have told thee that I have come to bring fire to the Earth, which is the same as descending so as to redeem the sins of the world through the fire.

And that is why Jesus repeated: If thou knew and were acquainted with the great gift of God, if thou perceived who it is that talks to thee and tells thee: Give me to drink, thou would beg me to give thee the eternal fountain that is a spring of sweet ambrosia and thou would convert thyself into the very fountain of life.

And He took the chalice, He blessed it and offered it to everyone, saying, "This is the Blood of the covenant that was shed for thee to redeem thee of sin and because of this, the spear was inserted into my rib, so that from my wound would flow Blood and Water."

And the great priest said to his brethren: Bring me fire and grapevines, and so they did. He then placed the sacrifice on the altar, a fountain of wine to his right and another one to his left, and a fountain of water in front of the wine.

And he put bread according to those who were listening to him. And the great priest kept himself dressed in white robes, which the Apostles imitated.

"This is my body, receive it for your redemption.

"This is my blood, receive it since it has been shed to redeem the world." - Excerpt from the Gnostic Mass

This is the message of Aquarius: this is the message of the new era.

And if any man shall take away from the words of the book of this prophecy, God shall take away his part out of the book of life, and out of the holy city, and from the things which are written in this book. He which testifieth these things saith, Surely, I come

quickly. Amen. Even so, come Lord Jesus. The grace of our Lord Jesus Christ be with you all. Amen.
- Revelation 22:19-21

Glossary

Absolute: Abstract space; that which is without attributes or limitations. Also known as sunyata, void, emptiness, Parabrahman, Adhi-buddha, and many other names. The Absolute has three aspects: the Ain, the Ain Soph, and the Ain Soph Aur.

"The Absolute is the Being of all Beings. The Absolute is that which Is, which always has Been, and which always will Be. The Absolute is expressed as Absolute Abstract Movement and Repose. The Absolute is the cause of Spirit and of Matter, but It is neither Spirit nor Matter. The Absolute is beyond the mind; the mind cannot understand It. Therefore, we have to intuitively understand Its nature." - Samael Aun Weor, *The Initiatic Path in the Arcana of Tarot and Kabbalah*

"In the Absolute we go beyond karma and the gods, beyond the law. The mind and the individual consciousness are only good for mortifying our lives. In the Absolute we do not have an individual mind or individual consciousness; there, we are the unconditioned, free and absolutely happy Being. The Absolute is life free in its movement, without conditions, limitless, without the mortifying fear of the law, life beyond spirit and matter, beyond karma and suffering, beyond thought, word and action, beyond silence and sound, beyond forms." - Samael Aun Weor, *The Major Mysteries*

Agni: (Sanskrit) One of the most ancient symbols in the world, representing the source and power of the sun, lightning, and fire. The Rig Veda states that all the Gods are centered in Agni (fire).

Ain Soph: "Ain Soph is the second aspect (of the Absolute); it is where a certain manifestation already exists... A divine Ray exists within the human being. That Ray wants to return back into its own Star that has always smiled upon it. The Star that guides our interior is a super divine Atom from the Abstract Absolute Space. The Kabbalistic name of that Atom is the sacred Ain Soph." - Samael Aun Weor, *The Initiatic Path in the Arcana of Tarot and Kabbalah*

Alchemy: Al (as a connotation of the Arabic word Allah: al-, the + ilah, God) means "The God." Also Al (Hebrew) for "highest" or El "God." Chem or Khem is from kimia (Greek) which means "to fuse or cast a metal." Also from Khem, the ancient name of Egypt. The synthesis is Al-Kimia: "to fuse with the highest" or "to fuse with God."

Arcanum: (Latin. plural: arcana). A secret or mystery known only to the specially educated. The root of the term "ark" as in the Ark of Noah and the Ark of the Covenent.

Arcanum A.Z.F.: The practice of sexual transmutation as couple (male-female), a technique known in Tantra and Alchemy. Arcanum refers to a hidden truth or law. A.Z.F. stands for A (agua, water), Z (azufre, sulfur), F (fuego, fire), and is thus: water + fire = consciousness. . Also, A (azoth =

chemical element that refers to fire). A & Z are the first and last letters of the alphabet thus referring to the Alpha & Omega (beginning & end).

Astral: This term is dervied from "pertaining to or proceeding from the stars," but in the esoteric knowledge it refers to the emotional aspect of the fifth dimension, which in Hebrew is called Hod.

Astral Body: The body utilized by the consciousness in the fifth dimension or world of dreams. What is commonly called the Astral Body is not the true Astral Body, it is rather the Lunar Protoplasmatic Body, also known as the Kama Rupa (Sanskrit, "body of desires") or "dream body" (Tibetan rmi-lam-gyi lus). The true Astral Body is Solar (being superior to Lunar Nature) and must be created, as the Master Jesus indicated in the Gospel of John 3:5-6, "Except a man be born of water and of the Spirit, he cannot enter into the kingdom of God. That which is born of the flesh is flesh; and that which is born of the Spirit is spirit." The Solar Astral Body is created as a result of the Third Initiation of Major Mysteries (Serpents of Fire), and is perfected in the Third Serpent of Light. In Tibetan Buddhism, the Solar Astral Body is known as the illusory body (sgyu-lus). This body is related to the emotional center and to the sephirah Hod.

"Really, only those who have worked with the Maithuna (White Tantra) for many years can possess the Astral Body." - Samael Aun Weor, *The Elimination of Satan's Tail*

Buddha: Literally, "awakened one." One of the Three Jewels (Tri-ratna). Commonly used to refer simply to the Buddha Shakyamuni (the "founder" of Buddhism), the term Buddha is actually a title. There are a vast number of Buddhas, each at different levels of attainment. At the ultimate level, a Buddha is a being who has become totally free of suffering. The Inner Being (Chesed) first becomes a Buddha when the Human Soul completes the work of the Fourth Initiation of Fire (related to Netzach, the mental body).

Centers, Seven: The human being has seven centers of psychological activity. The first five are the Intellectual, Emotional, Motor, Instinctive, and Sexual Centers. However, through inner development one learns how to utilize the Superior Emotional and Superior Intellectual Centers. Most people do not use these two at all.

Chakra: (Sanskrit) Literally, "wheel." The chakras are subtle centers of energetic transformation. There are hundreds of chakras in our hidden physiology, but seven primary ones related to the awakening of consciousness.

"The chakras are points of connection through which the divine energy circulates from one to another vehicle of the human being." - Samael Aun Weor, *Aztec Christic Magic*

Christ: Derived from the Greek Christos, "the Anointed One," and Krestos, whose esoteric meaning is "fire." The word Christ is a title, not a personal name.

"Indeed, Christ is a Sephirothic Crown (Kether, Chokmah and Binah) of incommensurable wisdom, whose purest atoms shine within Chokmah, the world of the Ophanim. Christ is not the Monad, Christ is not the Theosophical Septenary; Christ is not the Jivan-Atman. Christ is the Central Sun. Christ is the ray that unites us to the Absolute." - Samael Aun Weor, *The Initiatic Path in the Arcana of Tarot and Kabbalah*

"The Gnostic Church adores the Saviour of the World, Jesus. The Gnostic Church knows that Jesus incarnated Christ, and that is why they adore him. Christ is not a human nor a divine individual. Christ is a title given to all fully self-realised Masters. Christ is the Army of the Voice. Christ is the Verb. The Verb is far beyond the body, the soul and the Spirit. Everyone who is able to incarnate the Verb receives in fact the title of Christ. Christ is the Verb itself. It is necessary for everyone of us to incarnate the Verb (Word). When the Verb becomes flesh in us we speak with the verb of light. In actuality, several Masters have incarnated the Christ. In secret India, the Christ Yogi Babaji has lived for millions of years; Babaji is immortal. The Great Master of Wisdom Kout Humi also incarnated the Christ. Sanat Kumara, the founder of the Great College of Initiates of the White Lodge, is another living Christ. In the past, many incarnated the Christ. In the present, some have incarnated the Christ. In the future many will incarnate the Christ. John the Baptist also incarnated the Christ. John the Baptist is a living Christ. The difference between Jesus and the other Masters that also incarnated the Christ has to do with Hierarchy. Jesus is the highest Solar Initiate of the Cosmos..." - Samael Aun Weor, *The Perfect Matrimony*

Consciousness: "Wherever there is life, there exists the consciousness. Consciousness is inherent to life as humidity is inherent to water." - Samael Aun Weor, *Fundamental Notions of Endocrinology and Criminology*

From various dictionaries: 1. The state of being conscious; knowledge of one's own existence, condition, sensations, mental operations, acts, etc. 2. Immediate knowledge or perception of the presence of any object, state, or sensation. 3. An alert cognitive state in which you are aware of yourself and your situation. In Universal Gnosticism, the range of potential consciousness is allegorized in the Ladder of Jacob, upon which the angels ascend and descend. Thus there are higher and lower levels of consciousness, from the level of demons at the bottom, to highly realized angels in the heights.

"It is vital to understand and develop the conviction that consciousness has the potential to increase to an infinite degree." - The 14th Dalai Lama

"Light and consciousness are two phenomena of the same thing; to a lesser degree of consciousness, corresponds a lesser degree of light; to a greater degree of consciousness, a greater degree of light." - Samael Aun Weor, *The Esoteric Treatise of Hermetic Astrology*

Devi: "DEVI or Maheswari or Parasakti is the Supreme Sakti or Power of the Supreme Being. When Vishnu and Mahadeva destroyed various Asuras, the power of Devi was behind them. Devi took Brahma, Vishnu, and Rudra and gave them necessary Sakti to proceed with the work of creation, preservation, and destruction. Devi is the Creatrix of the universe. She is the Universal Mother. Durga, Kali, Bhagavati, Bhavani, Ambal, Ambika, Jagadamba, Kameswari, Ganga, Uma, Chandi, Chamundi, Lalita, Gauri,

Kundalini, Tara, Rajeswari, Tripurasundari, etc., are all Her forms. She is worshipped, during the nine days of the Dusserah as Durga, Lakshmi, and Saraswati. Devi is the Mother of all. The pious and the wicked, the rich and the poor, the saint and the sinner—all are Her children. Devi or Sakti is the Mother of Nature. She is Nature Itself. The whole world is Her body. Mountains are Her bones. Rivers are Her veins. Ocean is Her bladder. Sun, moon are Her eyes. Wind is Her breath. Agni is Her mouth. She runs this world show." - Swami Sivananda, *Devi*

Drukpa: (Also known variously as Druk-pa, Dugpa, Brugpa, Dag dugpa or Dad dugpa) A large sect which broke from the Kagyug-pa "the Ones of the Oral Tradition." They considered themselves as the heirs of the indian Gurus: their teaching, which goes back to Vajradhara, was conveyed through Dakini, from Naropa to Marpa and then to the ascetic and mystic poet Milarepa. Later on, Milarepa's disciples founded new monasteries, and new threads appeared, among which are the Karmapa and the Drukpa. All those schools form the Kagyug-pa order, in spite of episodic internal quarrels and extreme differences in practice.

The Drukpa sect is recognized by their ceremonial large red hats, but it should be known that they are not the only "Red Hat" group (the Nyingmas also use red hats). The Drukpas have established a particular worship of the Dorje (Vajra, or thunderbolt, a symbol of the phallus).

Samael Aun Weor wrote repeatedly in many books that the Drukpas practice and teach Black Tantrism, by means of the expelling of the sexual energy.

Ego: The multiplicity of contradictory psychological elements that we have inside are in their sum the "ego." Each one is also called "an ego" or an "I." Every ego is a psychological defect which produces suffering. The ego is three (related to our Three Brains or three centers of psychological processing), seven (capital sins), and legion (in their infinite variations).

"The ego is the root of ignorance and pain." - Samael Aun Weor, *The Esoteric Treatise of Hermetic Astrology*

"The Being and the ego are incompatible. The Being and the ego are like water and oil. They can never be mixed... The annihilation of the psychic aggregates (egos) can be made possible only by radically comprehending our errors through meditation and by the evident Self-reflection of the Being." - Samael Aun Weor, *The Pistis Sophia Unveiled*

Ens Seminis: (Latin) Literally, "the entity of semen." A term used by Paracelsus.

Gnosis: (Greek) Knowledge.

1. The word Gnosis refers to the knowledge we acquire through our own experience, as opposed to knowledge that we are told or believe in. Gnosis - by whatever name in history or culture - is conscious, experiential knowledge, not merely intellectual or conceptual knowledge, belief, or theory. This term is synonymous with the Hebrew "daath" and the Sanskrit "jna."

2. The tradition that embodies the core wisdom or knowledge of humanity.

"Gnosis is the flame from which all religions sprouted, because in its depth Gnosis is religion. The word "religion" comes from the Latin word "religare," which implies "to link the Soul to God"; so Gnosis is the very pure flame from where all religions sprout, because Gnosis is Knowledge, Gnosis is Wisdom." - Samael Aun Weor, *The Esoteric Path*

"The secret science of the Sufis and of the Whirling Dervishes is within Gnosis. The secret doctrine of Buddhism and of Taoism is within Gnosis. The sacred magic of the Nordics is within Gnosis. The wisdom of Hermes, Buddha, Confucius, Mohammed and Quetzalcoatl, etc., etc., is within Gnosis. Gnosis is the Doctrine of Christ." - Samael Aun Weor, *The Revolution of Beelzebub*

Heliogabalus Stone: A reference to the Cubic Stone of Yesod. Historically, a large black stone, a meteorite, that some describe from its image on coins and in sculpture as shaped like a bee-hive; others as phallic. This stone first appears in history atop its altar in the temple of Emesa on coins minted in the reign of Caracalla. It was taken by Varius Avitus Bassianus, Roman emperor (218-222), during his own reign, to Rome, and placed in a huge temple dedicated to it on the Palatine hill. Each summer, of the three he spent there, he led the stone in ceremonial procession, attended by musicians and dancers, to another palace in a garden at the outer edge of Rome. At the end of summer he would take it back to the Palatine. This is recorded in his coinage, as well as in the written sources. Varius was appointed priest of the sun-god Elagabal, whose name he adopted. Heliogabalus lived in Rome as an oriental despot and, giving himself up to detestable sensual pleasures, degraded the imperial office to the lowest point by most shameful vices, which had their origin in certain rites of oriental naturalistic religion.

Holy Spirit: "The Holy Spirit is the Fire of Pentecost or the fire of the Holy Spirit called Kundalini by the Hindus, the igneous serpent of our magical powers, Holy Fire symbolized by Gold..." - Samael Aun Weor, *The Perfect Matrimony*

"It has been said in The Divine Comedy with complete clarity that the Holy Spirit is the husband of the Divine Mother. Therefore, the Holy Spirit unfolds himself into his wife, into the Shakti of the Hindus. This must be known and understood. Some, when they see that the Third Logos is unfolded into the Divine Mother Kundalini, or Shakti, She that has many names, have believed that the Holy Spirit is feminine, and they have been mistaken. The Holy Spirit is masculine, but when He unfolds Himself into She, then the first ineffable Divine Couple is formed, the Creator Elohim, the Kabir, or Great Priest, the Ruach Elohim, that in accordance to Moses, cultivated the waters in the beginning of the world." - Samael Aun Weor, *The Initiatic Path in the Arcana of Tarot and Kabbalah*

Initiation: The process whereby the Innermost (the Inner Father) receives recognition, empowerment and greater responsibilities in the Internal Worlds, and little by little approaches His goal: complete Self-realization, or in other words, the return into the Absolute. Initiation NEVER applies to the "I" or our terrestrial personality.

"Nine Initiations of Minor Mysteries and seven great Initiations of Major Mysteries exist. The INNERMOST is the one who receives all of these Initiations. The Testament of Wisdom says: "Before the dawning of the false aurora upon the earth, the ones who survived the hurricane and the tempest were praising the INNERMOST, and the heralds of the aurora appeared unto them." The psychological "I" does not receives Initiations. The human personality does not receive anything. Nonetheless, the "I" of some Initiates becomes filled with pride when saying 'I am a Master, I have such Initiations.' Thus, this is how the "I" believes itself to be an Initiate and keeps reincarnating in order to "perfect itself", but, the "I" never ever perfects itself. The "I" only reincarnates in order to satisfy desires. That is all." - Samael Aun Weor, *The Aquarian Message*

Innermost: "Our real Being is of a universal nature. Our real Being is neither a kind of superior nor inferior "I." Our real Being is impersonal, universal, divine. He transcends every concept of "I," me, myself, ego, etc., etc." - Samael Aun Weor, *The Perfect Matrimony*

Also known as Atman, the Spirit, Chesed, our own individual interior divine Father.

"The Innermost is the ardent flame of Horeb. In accordance with Moses, the Innermost is the Ruach Elohim (the Spirit of God) who sowed the waters in the beginning of the world. He is the Sun King, our Divine Monad, the Alter-Ego of Cicerone." - Samael Aun Weor, *The Revolution of Beelzebub*

Internal Worlds: The many dimensions beyond the physical world. These dimensions are both subjective and objective. To know the objective internal worlds (the Astral Plane, or Nirvana, or the Klipoth) one must first know one's own personal, subjective internal worlds, because the two are intimately associated.

"Whosoever truly wants to know the internal worlds of the planet Earth or of the solar system or of the galaxy in which we live, must previously know his intimate world, his individual, internal life, his own internal worlds. Man, know thyself, and thou wilt know the Universe and its Gods. The more we explore this internal world called "myself," the more we will comprehend that we simultaneously live in two worlds, in two realities, in two confines: the external and the internal. In the same way that it is indispensable for one to learn how to walk in the external world so as not to fall down into a precipice, or not get lost in the streets of the city, or to select one's friends, or not associate with the perverse ones, or not eat poison, etc.; likewise, through the psychological work upon oneself we learn how to walk in the internal world, which is explorable only through Self-observation." - Samael Aun Weor, *Revolutionary Psychology*

Through the work in Self-observation, we develop the capacity to awaken where previously we were asleep: including in the objective internal worlds.

Jinn State: The condition that results from moving the physical body into the fourth dimension. "A body while in the "Jinn" state can float in the air (Laghima) or be submerged within the waters (Prakamya), or pass through fire without being burned, or be reduced to the size of an atom (Anima), or be enlarged to the point of touching the sun or the moon with the hand (Mahima). A body submerged within the supra-sensible worlds is submitted to the laws of those worlds. Then, this body is plastic and elastic, so it can change form, decrease its weight (Laghima), or increase its weight (Garima) willingly... When Jesus was walking upon the waters of the Sea of Galilee, he had his body in the state of "Jinn." Peter was able to liberate himself from the chains and to leave the prison, thanks to the assistance of an Angel who helped him place his body in the state of "Jinn."" - Samael Aun Weor, *The Aquarian Message*

Kabbalah: (Hebrew) Alternatively spelled Cabala, Qabalah (etc., ad nauseam) from the Hebrew KBLH or QBL, "to receive." An ancient esoteric teaching hidden from the uninitiated, whose branches and many forms have reached throughout the world. The true Kabbalah is the science and language of the Superior Worlds and is thus Objective, complete and without flaw; it is said that "All Enlightened Beings Agree," and their natural agreement is a function of the Awakened Consciousness. The Kabbalah is the language of that Consciousness, thus disagreement regarding it's meaning and interpretation is always due to the Subjective elements in the psyche.

"The objective of studying the Kabbalah is to be skilled for work in the Internal Worlds... One that does not comprehend remains confused in the Internal Worlds. Kabbalah is the basis in order to understand the language of these worlds." - Samael Aun Weor, *The Initiatic Path in the Arcana of Tarot and Kabbalah*

Kanda: "Prana circulates throughout all of our nadis and vital canals. All of the 72,000 nadis of our organism have their fundamental base on the nadi Kanda. The nadi Kanda is situated between the sexual organs and the anus. The Kanda collects all of the sexual energy that circulates throughout the 72,000 canals of our organism. The sexual energy is Prana, life. The Angel Aroch (Angel of Power) taught us the Pranava KANDIL, BANDIL, R for the awakening of Devi-Kundalini. These mantras act over the Kanda, reinforcing the vibration of Prana. Thus, the spouse of Shiva, who is coiled in the chakra Muladhara, is awakened when Prana is reinforced. The correct chanting pronunciation of this Pranava is as follows: KAN dil..... BAN dil..... Rrrrrrrrrr...... KAN is pronounced aloud. DIL is pronounced with a low voice. BAN is pronounced aloud. DIL is pronounced with a low voice. The letter R has to be rolled and acutely pronounced, imitating the sound produced by the rattles of the rattlesnake. This is how the Prana is reinforced, so that from the Kanda, from where the Shushumna nadi and the chakra Muladhara are joined, Devi-Kundalini awakens. The Kanda is precisely situated in the same point where the nadi Shushumna and the chakra Muladhara join. This is why the Pranava of the Angel Aroch acts so intensely over the Kundalini. The Kanda nourishes itself with the sexual organs. The Kanda has its physiological correspondence in the "cauda equina" of the spinal medulla... The Kanda is found situated within the chakra Muladhara." - Samael Aun Weor, *The Mysteries of the Fire: Kundalini Yoga*

Kundalini: "Kundalini, the serpent power or mystic fire, is the primordial energy or Sakti that lies dormant or sleeping in the Muladhara Chakra, the centre of the body. It is called the serpentine or annular power on account of serpentine form. It is an electric fiery occult power, the great pristine force which underlies all organic and inorganic matter. Kundalini is the cosmic power in individual bodies. It is not a material force like electricity, magnetism, centripetal or centrifugal force. It is a spiritual potential Sakti or cosmic power. In reality it has no form. [...] O Divine Mother Kundalini, the Divine Cosmic Energy that is hidden in men! Thou art Kali, Durga, Adisakti, Rajarajeswari, Tripurasundari, Maha-Lakshmi, Maha-Sarasvati! Thou hast put on all these names and forms. Thou hast manifested as Prana, electricity, force, magnetism, cohesion, gravitation in this universe. This whole universe rests in Thy bosom. Crores of salutations unto thee. O Mother of this world! Lead me on to open the Sushumna Nadi and take Thee along the Chakras to Sahasrara Chakra and to merge myself in Thee and Thy consort, Lord Siva. Kundalini Yoga is that Yoga which treats of Kundalini Sakti, the six centres of spiritual energy (Shat Chakras), the arousing of the sleeping Kundalini Sakti and its union with Lord Siva in Sahasrara Chakra, at the crown of the head. This is an exact science. This is also known as Laya Yoga. The six centres are pierced (Chakra Bheda) by the passing of Kundalini Sakti to the top of the head. 'Kundala' means 'coiled'. Her form is like a coiled serpent. Hence the name Kundalini." - Swami Sivananda, *Kundalini Yoga*

Laboratorium Oratorium: (Latin, indicating a place of work and prayer) A reference to the practice of Alchemy, originating from an illustration by Heinrich Kunrath.

Logos: (Greek) means Verb or Word. In Greek and Hebrew metaphysics, the unifying principle of the world. The Logos is the manifested deity of every nation and people; the outward expression or the effect of the cause which is ever concealed. (Speech is the "logos" of thought). The Logos has three aspects, known universally as the Trinity or Trimurti. The First Logos is the Father, Brahma. The Second Logos is the Son, Vishnu. The Third Logos is the Holy Spirit, Shiva. One who incarnates the Logos becomes a Logos.

"The Logos is not an individual. The Logos is an army of ineffable beings." - Samael Aun Weor, *Endocrinology & Criminology*

Magic: The word magic is derived from the ancient word "mag" that means priest. Real magic is the work of a priest. A real magician is a priest.

"Magic, according to Novalis, is the art of influencing the inner world consciously." - Samael Aun Weor, *The Mystery of the Golden Blossom*

"When magic is explained as it really is, it seems to make no sense to fanatical people. They prefer to follow their world of illusions." - Samael Aun Weor, *The Revolution of Beelzebub*

Major Mysteries: A series of initiations given to the Innermost Spirit after his Human Soul passes through successive trials and tests.

"There are nine Initiations of Minor Mysteries and five important Initiations of Major Mysteries. The Soul is the one who receives the initiations. This is a very intimate matter; something that one must not go about speaking of, nor something that must be told to anyone. Indeed, all the initiations and degrees that many schools of the physical world confer have no value whatsoever in the Superior Worlds, because the masters of the White Lodge only recognize the legitimate initiations of the Soul as genuine. These are completely internal. The disciple can ascend the nine Arcades, pass through all the nine Initiations of Minor Mysteries without having worked in the Arcanum A.Z.F. (Sexual Magic). Nevertheless, it is impossible to enter the Major Mysteries without Sexual Magic (the Arcanum A.Z.F.) In Egypt, everyone who reached the Ninth Sphere would inevitably receive by word of mouth the terrific secret of the great Arcanum (the most powerful Arcanum, the Arcanum A.Z.F.). The First Initiation is related with the first Serpent, the Second Initiation with the second Serpent, the Third Initiation with the third Serpent, the Fourth Initiation with the fourth Serpent, the Fifth Initiation with the fifth Serpent (the Sixth and Seventh belong to Buddhi, or Soul Consciousness and to Atman, or the Innermost of the human being)." - Samael Aun Weor, *The Perfect Matrimony*

Mantra: (Sanskrit, literally "mind protection") A sacred word or sound. The use of sacred words and sounds is universal throughout all religions and mystical traditions, because the root of all creation is in the Great Breath or the Word, the Logos. "In the beginning was the Word..."

Master: Like many terms related to spirituality, this one is grossly misunderstood. Samael Aun Weor wrote while describing the Germanic *Edda*, "In this Genesis of creation we discover Sexual Alchemy. The Fire fecundated the cold waters of chaos. The masculine principle Alfadur fecundated the feminine principle Niffleheim, dominated by Surtur (the Darkness), to bring forth life. That is how Ymir is born, the father of the giants, the Internal God of every human being, the Master." Therefore, the Master is the Innermost, Atman, the Father.

"The only one who is truly great is the Spirit, the Innermost. We, the intellectual animals, are leaves that the wind tosses about... No student of occultism is a Master. True Masters are only those who have reached the Fifth Initiation of Major Mysteries. Before the Fifth Initiation nobody is a Master." - Samael Aun Weor, *The Perfect Matrimony*

Meditation: "When the esotericist submerges himself into meditation, what he seeks is information." - Samael Aun Weor

"It is urgent to know how to meditate in order to comprehend any psychic aggregate, or in other words, any psychological defect. It is indispensable to know how to work with all our heart and with all our soul, if we want the elimination to occur." - Samael Aun Weor, *The Pistis Sophia Unveiled*

"1. The Gnostic must first attain the ability to stop the course of his thoughts, the capacity to not think. Indeed, only the one who achieves that capacity will hear the Voice of the Silence.

"2. When the Gnostic disciple attains the capacity to not think, then he must learn to concentrate his thoughts on only one thing.

"3. The third step is correct meditation. This brings the first flashes of the new consciousness into the mind.

"4. The fourth step is contemplation, ecstasy or Samadhi. This is the state of Turiya (perfect clairvoyance). - Samael Aun Weor, *The Perfect Matrimony*

Minerva: "Minerva, the goddess of wisdom, was the daughter of Jupiter. She was said to have leaped forth from his brain, mature, and in complete armour. She presided over the useful and ornamental arts, both those of men- such as agriculture and navigation- and those of women,- spinning, weaving, and needlework. She was also a warlike divinity; but it was defensive war only that she patronized, and she had no sympathy with Mars's savage love of violence and bloodshed. Athens was her chosen seat, her own city, awarded to her as the prize of a contest with Neptune, who also aspired to it, The tale ran that in the reign of Cecrops, the first king of Athens, the two deities contended for the possession of the city. The gods decreed that it should be awarded to that one who produced the gift most useful to mortals. Neptune gave the horse; Minerva produced the olive. The gods gave judgment that the olive was the more useful of the two, and awarded the city to the goddess; and it was named after her, Athens, her name in Greek being Athene." - Bullfinch's Mythology

Monad: (Latin) From monas, "unity; a unit, monad." The Monad is the Being, the Innermost, our own inner Spirit.

"We must distinguish between Monads and Souls. A Monad, in other words, a Spirit, is; a Soul is acquired. Distinguish between the Monad of a world and the Soul of a world; between the Monad of a human and the Soul of a human; between the Monad of an ant and the Soul of an ant. The human organism, in final synthesis, is constituted by billions and trillions of infinitesimal Monads. There are several types and orders of primary elements of all existence, of every organism, in the manner of germs of all the phenomena of nature; we can call the latter Monads, employing the term of Leibnitz, in the absence of a more descriptive term to indicate the simplicity of the simplest existence. An atom, as a vehicle of action, corresponds to each of these genii or Monads. The Monads attract each other, combine, transform themselves, giving form to every organism, world, micro-organism, etc. Hierarchies exist among the Monads; the Inferior

Monads must obey the Superior ones that is the Law. Inferior Monads belong to the Superior ones. All the trillions of Monads that animate the human organism have to obey the owner, the chief, the Principal Monad. The regulating Monad, the Primordial Monad permits the activity of all of its subordinates inside the human organism, until the time indicated by the Law of Karma." - Samael Aun Weor, *The Esoteric Treatise of Hermetic Astrology*

"(The number) one is the Monad, the Unity, Iod-Heve or Jehovah, the Father who is in secret. It is the Divine Triad that is not incarnated within a Master who has not killed the ego. He is Osiris, the same God, the Word." - Samael Aun Weor, *The Initiatic Path in the Arcana of Tarot and Kabbalah*

"When spoken of, the Monad is referred to as Osiris. He is the one that has to Self-realize Himself... Our own particular Monad needs us and we need it. Once, while speaking with my Monad, my Monad told me, 'I am self-realizing Thee; what I am doing, I am doing for Thee.' Otherwise, why are we living? The Monad wants to Self-realize and that is why we are here. This is our objective." - Samael Aun Weor, *The Initiatic Path in the Arcana of Tarot and Kabbalah*

"The Monads or Vital Genii are not exclusive to the physical organism; within the atoms of the Internal Bodies there are found imprisoned many orders and categories of living Monads. The existence of any physical or supersensible, Angelic or Diabolical, Solar or Lunar body, has billions and trillions of Monads as their foundation." - Samael Aun Weor, *The Esoteric Treatise of Hermetic Astrology*

Philosophical Stone: An Alchemical symbol of the Intimate Christ dressed with bodies of Gold. When acquired, this stone gives powers over nature. It is lost when thrown in water (through fornication). When the stone is dissolved in (sexual) water, then the metallic Spirit is melted, and interior Magnes escapes. It is said when this happens, one dissolves the stone in water on Saturday (Saturn = death). The Philosophical Stone is passes through phases of development: black, red & white. It is also the Cubic stone of Yesod (Parsifal Unveiled), the stone that Jacob anointed with oil and "a Stone of stumbling, a rock of offense."

Nicolas Valois: "It is a Stone of great virtue, and is called a Stone and is not a stone."

Samadhi: (Sanskrit) Literally means "union" or "combination" and its Tibetan equivilent means "adhering to that which is profound and definitive," or ting nge dzin, meaning "To hold unwaveringly, so there is no movement." Related terms include satori, ecstasy, manteia, etc. Samadhi is a state of consciousness. In the west, the term is used to describe an ecstatic state of consciousness in which the Essence escapes the painful limitations of the mind (the "I") and therefore experiences what is real: the Being, the Great Reality. There are many levels of Samadhi. In the sutras and tantras the term Samadhi has a much broader application whose precise interpretation depends upon which school and teaching is using it.

"Ecstasy is not a nebulous state, but a transcendental state of wonderment, which is associated with perfect mental clarity." - Samael Aun Weor, *The Elimination of Satan's Tail*

Satan: (Hebrew, opposer, or adversary) Is the fallen Lucifer, who is born within the psyche of every human being by means of the sexual impulse that culminates in the orgasm or sexual spasm of the fornicators. Satan, the fallen Lucifer directs the lustful animal currents towards the atomic infernos of the human being, thus it becomes the profoundly evil adversary of our Innermost (God) and human values within our own psyche. This is why it is often identified with the leader of the fallen angels or fallen human values (parts) of our consciousness trapped within the animal mind (legions of egos, defects, vices of the mind) in other words, Satan is the Devil or "evil" adversary of God "Good" that every body carries within their own psychological interior.

Second Death: The complete dissolution of the ego in the infernal regions of nature, which in the end (after unimaginable quantities of suffering) purifies the Essence of all sin (karma) so that it may try again to reach complete development.

"He that overcometh (the sexual passion) shall inherit all things; and I will be his God (I will incarnate myself within him), and he shall be my son (because he is a Christified one), But the fearful (the tenebrous, cowards, unbelievers), and unbelieving, and the abominable, and murderers, and whoremongers, and sorcerers, and idolaters, and all liars, shall have their part in the lake which burneth with fire and brimstone: which is the second death. (Revelation 21) This lake which burns with fire and brimstone is the lake of carnal passion. This lake is related with the lower animal depths of the human being and its atomic region is the abyss. The tenebrous slowly disintegrate themselves within the abyss until they die. This is the second death." - Samael Aun Weor, *The Aquarian Message*

Self-observation: An exercise of attention, in which one learns to become an indifferent observer of one's own psychological process. True Self-observation is an active work of directed attention, without the interference of thought.

"We need attention intentionally directed towards the interior of our own selves. This is not a passive attention. Indeed, dynamic attention proceeds from the side of the observer, while thoughts and emotions belong to the side which is observed." - Samael Aun Weor, *Revolutionary Psychology*

Self-realization: The achievement of perfect knowledge. This phrase is better stated as, "The realization of the Innermost Self," or "The realization of the true nature of self." At the ultimate level, this is the experiential, conscious knowledge of the Absolute, which is synonymous with Emptiness, Shunyata, or Non-being.

Self-remembering: A state of active consciousness, controlled by will, that begins with awareness of being here and now. This state has many levels (see: Consciousness). True Self-remembering occurs without thought or mental processing: it is a state of conscious perception and includes the remembrance of the inner Being.

Semen: The sexual energy of any creature or entity. In Gnosis, "semen" is a term used for the sexual energy of both masculine and feminine bodies. English semen originally meant 'seed of male animals' in the 14th century, and it was not applied to human males until the 18th century. It came from Latin semen, "seed of plants," from serere `to sow.' The Latin goes back to the Indo-European root *se-, source of seed, disseminate, season, seminar, and seminal. The word seminary (used for religious schools) is derived from semen and originally meant 'seedbed.'

That the semen is the source of all virtue is known from the word "seminal," derived from the Latin "semen," and which is defined as "highly original and influencing the development of future events: a seminal artist; seminal ideas."

In the esoteric tradition of pure sexuality, the word semen refers to the sexual energy of the organism, whether male or female. This is because male and female both carry the "seed" within: in order to create, the two "seeds" must be combined.

Sephirah: (Hebrew) plural: Sephiroth. literally, "jewel."

1. An emanation of Deity.

"The Ten Sephiroth of universal vibration emerge from the Ain Soph, which is the Microcosmic Star that guides our interior. This Star is the Real Being of our Being. Ten Sephiroth are spoken of, but in reality there are Twelve; the Ain Soph is the eleventh, and its tenebrous antithesis is in the Abyss, which is the twelfth Sephirah. These are twelve spheres or universal regions which mutually penetrate and co-penetrate without confusion." - Samael Aun Weor, *The Initiatic Path in the Arcana of Tarot and Kabbalah*

2. A name of the Divine Mother.

Sexual Magic: The word magic is dervied from the ancient word magos "one of the members of the learned and priestly class," from O.Pers. magush, possibly from PIE *magh- "to be able, to have power." [Quoted from On-line Etymology Dictionary].

"All of us possess some electrical and magnetic forces within, and, just like a magnet, we exert a force of attraction and repulsion... Between lovers that magnetic force is particularly powerful and its action has a far-reaching effect. - Samael Aun Weor, *The Mystery of the Golden Blossom*

Sexual magic refers to an ancient science that has been known and pro-tected by the purest, most spiritually advanced human beings, whose pur-pose and goal is the harnessing and perfection of our sexual forces. A more accurate translation of sexual magic would be "sexual priesthood."

In ancient times, the priest was always accompanied by a priestess, for they represent the divine forces at the base of all creation: the masculine and feminine, the Yab-Yum, Ying-Yang, Father-Mother: the Elohim.

Unfortunately, the term "sexual magic" has been grossly misinterpreted by mistaken persons such as Aleister Crowley, who advocated a host of degenerated practices, all of which belong solely to the lowest and most perverse mentality. This website and the teachings presented here reject all such philosophies, theories, and practices, for they lead only to the enslavement of the consciousness, the worship of lust and desire, and the decay of humanity.

True, upright, heavenly sexual magic is the natural harnessing of our latent forces, making them active and harmonious with nature and the divine.

"People are filled with horror when they hear about sexual magic; however, they are not filled with horror when they give themselves to all kinds of sexual perversion and to all kinds of carnal passion." - Samael Aun Weor, *The Perfect Matrimony*

Solar Bodies: The physical, vital, astral, mental, and casual bodies that are created through the beginning stages of Alchemy/Tantra and that provide a basis for existence in their corresponding levels of nature, just as the physical body does in the physical world. These bodies or vehicles are superior due to being created out of Solar (Christic) Energy, as opposed to the inferior, lunar bodies we receive from nature. Also known as the Wedding Garment (Christianity), the Merkabah (Kabbalah), To Soma Heliakon (Greek), and Sahu (Egyptian).

"All the Masters of the White Lodge, the Angels, Archangels, Thrones, Seraphim, Virtues, etc., etc., etc. are garbed with the Solar Bodies. Only those who have Solar Bodies have the Being incarnated. Only someone who possesses the Being is an authentic Human Being." - Samael Aun Weor, *The Esoteric Treatise of Hermetic Astrology*

Tantra: Sanskrit for "continuum" or "unbroken stream." This refers first (1) to the continuum of vital energy that sustains all existence, and second (2) to the class of knowledge and practices that harnesses that vital energy, thereby transforming the practitioner. There are many schools of Tantrism, but they can be classified in three types: White, Grey and Black. Tantra has long been known in the West as Alchemy.

"In the view of Tantra, the body's vital energies are the vehicles of the mind. When the vital energies are pure and subtle, one's state of mind will be accordingly affected. By transforming these bodily energies we transform the state of consciousness." - The 14th Dalai Lama

Tarot: "Through the Gypsies the Tarot cards may be traced back to the religious symbolism of the ancient Egyptians. [...] Court de Gébelin believed the word Tarot itself to be derived from two Egyptian words, Tar, meaning "road," and Ro, meaning "royal." Thus the Tarot constitutes the royal road to wisdom. (See Le Monde Primitif.) [...] The Tarot is undoubtedly a vital element in Rosicrucian symbolism, possibly the very book of universal knowledge which the members of the order claimed to possess. The Rota Mundi is a term frequently occurring in the early manifestoes of the Fraternity of the Rose Cross. The word Rota by a rearrangement of its letters becomes Taro, the ancient name of these mysterious cards. [...] The Pythagorean numerologist will also find an important relationship to exist between the numbers on the cards and the designs accompanying the numbers. The Qabbalist will be immediately impressed by the significant sequence of the cards, and the alchemist will discover certain emblems meaningless save to one versed in the divine chemistry of transmutation and regeneration.' As the Greeks placed the letters of their alphabet--with their corresponding numbers--upon the various parts of the body of their humanly represented Logos, so the Tarot cards have an analogy not only in the parts and members of the universe but also in the divisions of the human body.. They are in fact the key to the magical constitution of man. [...] The Tarot cards must be considered (1) as separate and complete hieroglyphs, each representing a distinct principle, law, power, or element in Nature; (2) in relation to each other as the effect of one agent operating upon another; and (3) as vowels and consonants of a philosophic alphabet. The laws governing all phenomena are represented by the symbols upon the Tarot cards, whose numerical values are equal to the numerical equivalents of the phenomena. As every structure consists of certain elemental parts, so the Tarot cards represent the components of the structure of philosophy. Irrespective of the science or philosophy with which the student is working, the Tarot cards can be identified with the essential constituents of his subject, each card thus being related to a specific part according to mathematical and philosophical laws. "An imprisoned person," writes Eliphas Levi, "with no other book than the Tarot, if he knew how to use it, could in a few years acquire universal knowledge, and would be able to speak on all subjects with unequalled learning and inexhaustible eloquence." - Manly P. Hall, *The Secret Teachings of All Ages* (1928)

Tattva: (Sanskrit) "truth, fundamental principle." A reference to the essential nature of a given thing. Tattvas are the elemental forces of nature. There are numerous systems presenting varying tattvas as fundamental principles of nature. Gnosticism utilizes a primary system of five: akash (which is the elemental force of the ether), tejas (fire), vayu (air), apas (water), and prittvi (earth). Two higher tattvas are also important: adi and samadhi.

Vestal: A term derived from Roman religion, referring to a priestess of Vesta. The term refers to a sacred duty performed by virginal women in many esoteric traditions. In Roman times, while still little girls, they were chosen from prominent Roman families. Their duties included the preparation of sacrifices and the tending of the sacred fire. If any vestal broke her vow of chastity, it is said that she was entombed alive. The vestals had great influence in the Roman state. Their primary duty was to work in the sacred practice of Alchemy with the Initiates of the temple. The use of Vestals is no longer lawful and is not a part of any White Tradition in these times.

Vital Body: (Also called Ethereal Body) The superior aspect of the physical body, composed of the energy or vital force that provides life to the physical body.

"It is written that the vital body or the foundation of organic life within each one of us has four ethers. The chemical ether and the ether of life are related with chemical processes and sexual reproduction. The chemical ether is a specific foundation for the organic chemical phenomena. The ether of life is the foundation of the reproductive and transformative sexual processes of the race. The two superior ethers, luminous and reflective, have more elevated functions. The luminous ether is related with the caloric, luminous, perceptive, etc., phenomena. The reflective ether serves as a medium of expression for willpower and imagination." - Samael Aun Weor, *The Pistis Sophia Unveiled*

In Tibetan Buddhism, the vital body is known as the subtle body (lus phra-mo).

Vulcan: The Latin or Roman name for the Greek God Hephaistos, known by the Egyptians as Ptah. A God of fire with a deep and ancient mythology, commonly remembered as the blacksmith who forges weapons for Gods and heroes.

Quotes from Paracelsus: "The office of Vulcan is the separation of the good from the bad. So the Art of Vulcan, which is Alchemy, is like unto death, by which the eternal and the temporal are divided one from another. So also this art might be called the death of things." - De Morbis Metallicis, Lib. I., Tract III., c. 1. "Vulcan is an astral and not a corporal fabricator." - De Caduco Matricis, Par. VI. "The artist working in metals and other minerals transforms them into other colours, and in so doing his operation is like that of the heaven itself. For as the artist excocts by means of Vulcan, or the igneous element, so heaven performs the work of coction through the Sun. The Sun, therefore, is the Vulcan of heaven accomplishing coction in the earth." - De Icteritiis. "Vulcan is the fabricator and architect of all things, nor is his habitation in heaven only, that is, in the firmament, but equally in all the other elements." - Lib. Meteorum, c. 4. "Where the three prime principles are wanting, there also the igneous essence is absent. The Igneous Vulcan is nothing else but Sulphur, Sal Nitrum, and Mercury." - Ibid., c.5.

Yoga: (Sanskrit) "union." Similar to the Latin "religare," the root of the word "religion." In Tibetan, it is "rnal-'byor" which means "union with the fundamental nature of reality."

"The word YOGA comes from the root Yuj which means to join, and in its spiritual sense, it is that process by which the human spirit is brought into near and conscious communion with, or is merged in, the Divine Spirit, according as the nature of the human spirit is held to be separate from (Dvaita, Visishtadvaita) or one with (Advaita) the Divine Spirit." - Swami Sivananda, *Kundalini Yoga*

"Patanjali defines Yoga as the suspension of all the functions of the mind. As such, any book on Yoga, which does not deal with these three aspects of the subject, viz., mind, its functions and the method of suspending them, can he safely laid aside as unreliable and incomplete." - Swami Sivananda, *Practical Lessons In Yoga*

"The word yoga means in general to join one's mind with an actual fact..." - The 14th Dalai Lama

"The soul aspires for the union with his Innermost, and the Innermost aspires for the union with his Glorian." - Samael Aun Weor, *The Revolution of Beelzebub*

"All of the seven schools of Yoga are within Gnosis, yet they are in a synthesized and absolutely practical way. There is Tantric Hatha Yoga in the practices of the Maithuna (Sexual Magic). There is practical Raja Yoga in the work with the chakras. There is Gnana Yoga in our practices and mental disciplines which we have cultivated in secrecy for millions of years. We have Bhakti Yoga in our prayers and Rituals. We have Laya Yoga in our meditation and respiratory exercises. Samadhi exists in our practices with the Maithuna and during our deep meditations. We live the path of Karma Yoga in our upright actions, in our upright thoughts, in our upright feelings, etc." - Samael Aun Weor, *The Revolution of Beelzebub*

"The Yoga that we require today is actually ancient Gnostic Christian Yoga, which absolutely rejects the idea of Hatha Yoga. We do not recommend Hatha Yoga simply because, spiritually speaking, the acrobatics of this discipline are fruitless; they should be left to the acrobats of the circus." - Samael Aun Weor, *The Yellow Book*

"Yoga has been taught very badly in the Western World. Multitudes of pseudo-sapient Yogis have spread the false belief that the true Yogi must be an infrasexual (an enemy of sex). Some of these false yogis have never even visited India; they are infrasexual pseudo-yogis. These ignoramuses believe that they are going to achieve in-depth realization only with the yogic exercises, such as asanas, pranayamas, etc. Not only do they have such false beliefs, but what is worse is that they propagate them; thus, they misguide many people away from the difficult, straight, and narrow door that leads unto the light. No authentically Initiated Yogi from India would ever think that he could achieve his inner self-realization with pranayamas or asanas, etc. Any legitimate Yogi from India knows very well that such yogic exercises are only co-assistants that are very useful for their health and for the development of their powers, etc. Only the Westerners and pseudo-yogis have within their minds the belief that they can achieve Self-realization with such exercises. Sexual Magic is practiced very secretly within the Ashrams of India. Any True Yogi Initiate from India works with the Arcanum A.Z.F. This is taught by the Great Yogis from India that have visited the Western world, and if it has not been taught by these great, Initiated Hindustani Yogis, if it has not been published in their books of Yoga, it was in order to avoid scandals. You can be absolutely sure that the Yogis who do not practice Sexual Magic will never achieve birth in the Superior Worlds. Thus, whosoever affirms the contrary is a liar, an impostor." - Samael Aun Weor, *The Esoteric Course of Kabbalah*

Yogi: (Sanskrit) male yoga practitioner.

Yogini: (Sanskrit) female yoga practitioner.

Index

Glorian Publishing is a non-profit publisher dedicated to spreading the sacred universal doctrine to suffering humanity. All of our works are made possible by the kindness and generosity of sponsors. If you would like to make a tax-deductible donation, you may send it to the address below, or visit our website for other alternatives. If you would like to sponsor the publication of a book, please contact us at 877-726-2359 or help@gnosticteachings.org.

Glorian Publishing
7420 SW Hunziker Rd Suite F
Portland, OR 97223 US
Phone: 877-726-2359 · Fax: 212-501-1676

VISIT US ONLINE AT:

glorian.info
gnosticbooks.org
gnosticteachings.org
gnosticradio.org
gnosticstore.org